D0857430

Soldier of the South

GENERAL AND MRS. PICKETT
From a miniature after a likeness taken about the
time of their marriage

SOLDIER OF THE SOUTH
GENERAL PICKETT'S WAR LETTERS TO HIS WIFE

EDITED BY

ARTHUR CREW INMAN

With Illustrations

 BOOKS FOR LIBRARIES PRESS
FREEPORT, NEW YORK

First Published 1928
Reprinted 1971

INTERNATIONAL STANDARD BOOK NUMBER:
0-8369-5854-3

LIBRARY OF CONGRESS CATALOG CARD NUMBER:
78-160986

PRINTED IN THE UNITED STATES OF AMERICA

O N the 1st, 2nd, and 3rd of July, 1863, at Gettys‑ burg, was fought the decisive battle in that long and fierce war between the United States of America and the Confederate States of America. No war in all history has been more bitterly and determinedly waged. The reasons which led up to the great struggle are variously stated by various historians. For what‑ ever reason begun, the so‑called 'Civil War' proved to be one of the most epic of all embattled conflicts in history or legend. Heroes walked the earth, men in gray and men in blue. But, since the men in gray were fighting — as they conscientiously and spiritedly be‑ lieved — for their own fields and firesides, for their sacred right to the institution of individual self‑ government, for the inviolability of their heritage, it was from among the r leaders that the most illustrious heroes came. Name them, — Lee, the two Johnstons, Jackson, Stuart, the two Hills, Beauregard, Forrest, Pickett, Early, Ewell, Ashby, Mosby, Hood, Wheel‑ er! Was ever a more gallant and legendary group of soldiers gathered together under one flag, to fight for one cause?

.　　.　　.　　.　　.　　.　　.　　.

It was on the third day of the fighting at Gettys-burg that upon General George E. Pickett was placed the responsibility his unfailing gallantry had earned for him, in the judgment of the man whom histo-rians term the greatest of all American soldiers, Gen-eral Robert E. Lee. George E. Pickett was the scion of an old tidewater Virginia family. He was born in Richmond, Virginia, January 25, 1825. He was a cadet at West Point from 1842-6. Serving consec-utively as Second Lieutenant and First Lieutenant, he was appointed Captain Ninth Infantry, United States Army, in 1855. He campaigned during the Mexican War, being engaged in most of the battles of that war. He was the first to scale the parapets of Chapultepec, and it was he who unfurled the flag over the Castle. After the Mexican War, he was variously on duty in Texas, Florida, Fortress Monroe, and Washington Territory. At the outbreak of the 'South-ern Rebellion', he resigned from the United States Army and took ship from Washington Territory to New York. From that metropolis he made his way

South to Virginia, where he immediately enlisted as a private. He was commissioned, the next day, Captain, and a short time later, Colonel. Early in 1862 he received his commission as Brigadier-General, and, soon after, as Major-General, in which latter capacity he served until the conclusion of the 'War'. He took part in the battles of Williamsburg, Seven Pines, Gaines's Mill, Fredericksburg. He was wounded at Gaines's Mill, and was absent from his command until September of the same year. He won distinction for himself in the capacity of leader, his superior officers believing in his ability and his men worshipping him as man and general. So it came to pass, then, that on that fateful day of July 3, 1863, the supreme honor of leading the crucial charge against the Federals was given by the Commanding-Officer to General Pickett. See him! A fine and gallant figure, astride his black war-horse, his blue eyes afire with ardor, his auburn hair bronzed to the sun, his flashing sabre in hand, he leads his men through the shell-scored wheat across the valley towards Cemetery Hill. In 'common' time they march, 'dressed' towards the center. Shrapnel, canister, and minie-balls decimate their ranks. But still they press on, shouting: "We'll follow you, Marse George! We'll follow you!" And follow him they did, on their triumphal charge across the golden pages of history! Nearly five thousand strong, they entered upon their march. The flag of Virginia was a moment unfurled upon the coveted Federal works. But no supporting columns followed. Judging from all existing evidence it would seem that General Longstreet had failed to notify the Commander of the dearth of ammunition; had failed to follow up General Pickett's charge with supporting brigades; had, in a word, lost for the South its immortal chance of gaining success and independence. Five thousand strong, the men of General Pickett's Division set forth across the field of their glory and their death. Not one thousand five hundred returned. Ah, the tragedy; ah, the wonder; ah, the eternal fame — of that charge!

. . . .

The letters in this volume were written by General Pickett to La Salle Corbell Pickett, his bride and his wife, during the period of the 'War', and after. Yellow pages, bearing, nearly all, a 'London' imprint; yellow pages, crisp with age, carrying down through unrolling years, in neatly-penciled or penned sentences, the flavor of the past, romantic, glamorous, sad, gay, tender, sweetly sentimental, imbued with unquestioning faith in Almighty God, in Virginia, in honor, and in the brave young 'war'bride' of his love.

. . . .

Every attempt has been made to adhere scrupu' lously to the exact historical statements contained in these letters, leaving them strictly as they were written. Otherwise, where the message is personal rather than historical, an over'long sentence has been broken up into two, punctuation inserted in the style of the author, an 'and' put in or omitted, a word that the passage of years has given another meaning replaced by one synonymous.

. . . .

Most of these letters, before they appeared in book form in 1913, under the title of 'The Heart of a Sol' dier', were published in 'McClure's Magazine.' They were, I believe, originally edited by Mr. McClure. I wish to acknowledge a debt to his excellent judg' ment. I wish to express my thanks to Mr. Ferris Greenslet for his coöperation. And, above all else, I desire to express to Mrs. General George E. Pickett my deep appreciation for the privilege which she has

FOREWORD

accorded me in allowing me to examine, select, and edit, the personal correspondence of her 'Soldier'.

* * * * * * * *

To the undying spirit of the soldiers of the 'Old South' may I dedicate this volume. May it stand as one eternal symbol of their courage, their devotion, their grace, their heroism, a symbol to inspire the future of all mankind to walk in the humility of in⁄nate nobility that was theirs.

ARTHUR CREW INMAN

BOSTON, 1928

CONTENTS

CONTENTS

CONTENTS

ILLUSTRATIONS

GENERAL PICKETT'S LETTERS
TO HIS WIFE

I

*In which Captain Pickett Tells why he Sided
with the South*

SEVERAL weeks ago I wrote quite a long letter
from far-away San Francisco to a very dear little
girl, and told her that a certain soldier who wears one of
her long, silken ringlets next his heart was homeward
bound, and that he hoped a line of welcome would
meet him on his arrival in his native state. He told
her of the difficulties he had experienced in being relieved from his post, of how sorry he was to sheathe
the sword which had helped to bring victory to the
country for which he had fought, and how sorry he
was to say good-by to his little command and to part
from his faithful and closest companion, his dog,
and his many dear friends; but sorrier still for the
existing circumstances which made this severance
necessary. He told her many things for which, with
him, she will be sorry, and some of which he hopes
will make her glad. He is troubled by finding no an-

swer to this long letter which, having at that time no notion of the real conditions here, he is afraid was written too freely by far.

No, my child, I had no conception of the intensity of feeling, the bitterness and hatred toward those who were so lately our friends and are now our enemies. I, of course, have always strenuously opposed disunion, not as doubting the right of secession, which was taught in our text-book at West Point, but as gravely questioning its expediency. I believed that the revolutionary spirit which infected both North and South was but a passing phase of fanaticism which would perish under the rebuke of all good citizens, who would surely unite in upholding the Constitution; but when that great assembly, composed of ministers, lawyers, judges, chancellors, statesmen, mostly white haired men of thought, met in South Carolina and when their districts were called crept noiselessly to the table in the center of the room and affixed their signatures to the parchment on which the ordinance of secession was inscribed, and when in deathly silence, in spite of the gathered multitude, General Jamison arose and without preamble read: "The ordinance of secession has been signed and

ratified; I proclaim the State of South Carolina an in-
dependent sovereignty," and lastly, when my old boy-
hood's friend called for an invasion, it was evident that
both the advocates and opponents of secession had read
the portents aright.

You know, my little lady, some of those cross-
stitched mottoes on the cardboard samplers which
used to hang on my nursery wall, such as, "He who
provides not for his own household is worse than an
infidel," and "Charity begins at home," made a last-
ing impression upon me; and while I love my neighbor, i.e., my country, I love my household, i.e., my
state, *more*, and I could not be an infidel and lift my
sword against my own kith and kin, even though I
do believe, my most wise little counselor and confi-
dante, that the measure of American greatness can be
achieved only under one flag, and I fear, alas, there
can never again reign for either of us the true spirit
of national unity, whether divided and under two
flags, or united under one.

We did not tarry even for a day in 'Frisco, but under
assumed names my friend, Sam Barron, and I sailed
for New York, where we arrived on the very day that

Sam's father, Commodore Barron, was brought there, a prisoner, which fact was proclaimed aloud by the pilot amid cheers of the passengers and, upon our landing, heralded by the newsboys with more cheers. Poor Sam had a hard fight to hide his feelings and to avoid arrest. We separated, as mere ship acquaintances, and went by different routes to meet again, as arranged, at the house of Doctor Paxton, a Southern sympathizer and our friend.

As I was walking up from the dock a stranger rather roughly jostled against me, saying "I beg your pardon, sir, but you've dropped your pocketbook." I was about to resent this intrusion and disown the purse when a telegraphic expression on the stranger's face made me suddenly change my mind, and, carelessly putting the purse into my pocket, I thanked him and made for the bus. Opening the purse to pay my fare I found a roll of bank notes, some silver, several clippings and a very much soiled card of a New York hostelry, and across this worn and greasy card, in the well known hand of an old friend and comrade, were some very pertinent lines written in Chinook jargon and labeled in English : — "This is a part of a copy of a letter written to me by my Indian sweetheart." Now, Bright-Eyes, that you may not be jealous, and that you may know how loyal and unself-ish and generous a brother officer can be, even though he may differ from you in principles, and is fighting against you and your flag, I will copy this alleged 'love-letter', its literal translation:

Ah you've come. I too have just arrived. You look out. The bald eagle cries out. No you go friend's house. Understand? Rattle snakes everywhere. Steal away at once. Make haste. Everybody watches. Get out. That is best. I no idle talk. Escape or you a pris-oner. This money is a present for you. I love you. Send away fear. From you all evil.

Yours very well -

Now, Chula, Carissima, was not that a 'for-truly' love-letter. It was well that we obeyed to the letter its injunctions, "Kah-kwah spose", for the "friend's house" and his friends' homes were searched during the night while we were concealed in a neighbor's stable.

On the next day we left for Canada by the earliest train. Thence we made our perilous way through Kentucky to Tennessee, barely escaping arrest several times, and finally arrived in dear old Richmond, September 13th, just four days ago. I at once enlisted in the army and the following day was commissioned Captain. But so bitter is the feeling here that my being unavoidably delayed so long in avowing my allegiance to my state has been most cruelly and severely criticized by friends, yes, and even relatives — near relatives, too.

Now, little one, if you had the very faintest idea how happy a certain captain in the C. S. A. would be to look into your beautiful, soul-speaking eyes and hear your wonderfully musical voice, I think you would let him know by wire where he could find you. I shall almost listen for the electricity which says, "I am at ———. Come." I know that you will have mercy on your devoted

Soldier

Richmond, September 17, 1861

II

Written after a Light Skirmish with the Enemy

YOUR welcome note gladdened my drooping spirits last evening. How can I thank you for the token? I shall always cherish it, my darling. I sent a short note to you, via Petersburg, to Wakefield. I sincerely trust you received it, as in it I advised you not to come down into this part of the country. The Yankees are burning everything they can reach, and God only knows what excesses they may commit on the defenseless, should they have the power. So much troubled am I about you, that I send this by a courier of my own, that he may deliver it to you in person (how I wish I were the courier!). I'm afraid you will only expose yourself needlessly to harm. I don't know when I shall see you, but I should be nearly as far from you as at present. At any rate, I should be worse than miserable did I know you were so near these now ap-parently infuriated beings.

Alas, my darling, as the Indian says when despond-ent, "My heart is on the ground." The enemy has been strongly reënforced, and the town is one network of batteries and entrenchments. I have had two little brushes with them, running them into their works both times—the first one yesterday week. I was ordered to make a reconnaissance in force, which was done by a part of Armistead's Brigade, and in so doing we got under a concentrated fire of about sixteen guns and had as jolly a little time of it for about fifteen minutes as I ever saw. Parrot and round shot were about as thick as the ticks are, and their name is legion. However, the object was effected, and we have lost altogether only about seventy-five men from my division.

Haven't you some relatives living this side of the Blackwater—a Captain Phillips of the 3rd? Write me, my dearest. Two long, weary weeks since I drank comfort from those bright eyes—to me a *year* of anxiety.

Your devoted and miserable

Soldier

New Somerton Road, April 21, 1862

III

Concerning Legitimate Warfare, Secession, and the
Mishaps of an Old Major of Artillery

MY heart beat with joy this morning, my dar/
ling, when Captain Peacock returned to camp,
bringing me your beautiful letter — beautiful because
it was the echo of a pure spirit and a radiant soul. I am
humbly grateful, my little sweetheart, for this loyal
devotion which you give me — your soldier. Let us
pray to our dear Heavenly Father to spare us to each
other and give us strength to bear cheerfully this en/
forced separation. I know that it cannot be long, and
that sooner or later our flag will float over the seas of
the world, for our cause is right and just.

Why, my Sallie, all that we ask is a separation from
people of contending interests, who love us as a nation
as little as we love them, the dissolution of a union
which has lost its holiness, to be let alone and per/
mitted to sit under our own vine and fig tree and eat
our figs peeled or dried or fresh or pickled, just as we
choose. The enemy is our enemy because he neither
knows nor understands us, and yet, hating us, will not
let us part in peace and be neighbors, but insists on
fighting us to make us one with him, forgetting that

9

both slavery and secession were his own institutions. The North is fighting for the Union, and we—for home and fireside. All the men I know and love in the world—comrades and friends, both North and South—are exposed to hardships and dangers, and are fighting on one side or the other, and each for that which he knows to be right.

Speaking of fighting, Captain Peacock this morn' ing brings us the news that the daring, fearless —— has again won—shall I say, a victory? No, not vic' tory. Victory is such a glorious, triumphant word. I cannot use it in speaking of warfare that is illegal to many of us. Marse Robert's* approval and commenda' tion of this illegitimate mode is a source of surprise, for, like many of us, the dear old " Tyee " was reared and schooled in honorable warfare.

Well, as Trenholm said, only those who have en' listed for this whole war, with muskets on their shoul' ders and knapsacks on their backs, have a right to crit' icize; but I reserve even from these the right, and acknowledge myself wrong in criticizing. An old army story, though hardly illustrative enough to be justifiable in telling, occurs to me:

An old major of artillery, who was always deploring

* General Lee.

the fact that he couldn't use his own favorite arm against the Indians, determined one day to try the *moral* effect of it upon a tribe of friendly ones nearby. So he took one of the small howitzers which defended the fort and securely strapped it to the back of an army mule, with the muzzle projecting over the mule's tail, and then proceeded with the captain, sergeant and orderly to the bluff on the bank of the Missouri where the Indians were encamped. The gun was loaded and primed, the fuse inserted and the mule backed to the very edge of the bluff.

The mule with his wonted curiosity, hearing the fizzing, turned his head to see what unusual thing was happening to him. The next second his feet were bunched up together, making forty revolutions a min- ute, the gun threatening with instant destruction everything within a radius of five miles. The captain climbed a tree, the sergeant and orderly following suit. The fat major, too heavy to climb, rolled over on the ground, alternately praying to God and cursing the mule. When the explosion came, the recoil of the gun and the wild leap of the terrified mule carried both over the bluff and to the bottom of the river. The cap- tain, the sergeant, and the poor, crestfallen, discom- fited major, with the mule and the gun to account for, returned to the fort, soon to be waited on by the Indian chiefs, who had held a hurried council. The high chief, bowing his head up and down, said:

"Injun go home. Injun ver' brave. Injun love white man. Injun help white man. Injun heap use gun, use knife, heap use bow-arrow; but when white man shoot off whole jackass, Injun no think right— no can understand. Injun no help white man fight that way. Injun go home."

So, my Sallie, if you will forgive your soldier for telling this old-time story, and let him say that he does not approve of fighting in the way in which——fights, he will bid you good-by and eat his breakfast, which the cook says is getting cold. Will you come, my darling, and have some coffee with your soldier? It is some we captured, and is *real* coffee.

Come! The tin cup is clean and shining; but the corn-bread is greasy and smoked. And the bacon— that is greasy, too. But it is good, and tastes all right, if it will only hold out till our Stars and Bars wave over the land of the free and the home of the brave, and we have our own home. Nevermore, then, we'll hear of wars, but only of love and of life with its eternal joys.

Your own

Soldier

Headquarters, May —, 1862

IV

In which are Given Certain Important Details of the Battle of Seven Pines

A VIOLENT storm was raging, flooding the level ground, as I wrote you last, followed the next day by one of fire and blood — the Battle of Seven Pines.

I pray, my prettice, that you accepted the invitation of your mountain chum, and that your beautiful eyes and tender heart have been spared the horrors of war which this battle must have poured into sad Richmond. Three hundred and fifty of your soldier's brigade, 1700 strong, were killed or wounded, and all fought as Virginians should, fighting as they did for the right, for love, honor, home and state — principles which they had been taught from the mothers' knees, the schoolroom and the pulpit.

Under orders from Old Peter,* we marched at daylight and reported to D. H. Hill, near Seven Pines. Hill directed me to ride over and communicate with Hood. I started at once with Charlie and Archer, of my staff, to obey this order, but had gone only a short distance when we met a part of the Louisiana Zou-

---

* General Longstreet.

13

aves, in panic. I managed to seize and detain one fellow, mounted on a mule that seemed to have imbibed
his rider's fear and haste. The man dropped his plun-
der and seizing his carbine threatened to kill me unless I released him at once, saying that the Yankees
were upon his heels. We galloped back to Hill's headquarters—Archer bringing up the rear with the
Zouave, who explained that the enemy were advanc-
ing in force and were within a few hundred yards of
us. Hill ordered me to attack at once, which I did,
driving them through an abatis over a crossroad leading to the railroad.

As we were nearing the second abatis, I, on foot
at the time, noticed that Armistead's Brigade had
broken, and sent a courier back posthaste to Hill for
troops. A second and third message were sent and
then a fourth, telling him that if he would send
me more troops and ammunition we could drive the
enemy across the Chickahominy. But alas, Hill, as
brave, as great, as heroic a soldier as he is, has, since
the fall of Johnston, been so bothered and annoyed
with countermanding orders that he was, if I may
say so, addled, confused. After this delay nothing was
left for us but to withdraw. Hill sent two regiments
of Colston's Brigade, and ordered Mahone's Brigade

on my right, and at one o'clock at night, under his orders, we withdrew in perfect form while the enemy retreated to their bosky cover.

Thus, my darling, was ended the Battle of Seven Pines. No shot was fired afterward. Oh, how I wish I could say it ended all battles and that the last shot that will ever be heard was fired on June first, 1862. What a change love does make! How tender all things become to a heart touched by love — how beautiful the beautiful is and how abhorrent is evil! See, my darling, see what power you have. Guard it well.

I have heard that my dear old friend, McClellan, is lying ill about ten miles from here. May some loving, soothing hand minister to him. He was, he is and he will always be, even were his pistol pointed at my heart, my dear, loved friend. May God bless him and spare his life. You, my darling, may not be in sympathy with this feeling, for I know you see 'no good in Nazareth.' Forgive me for feeling differently from you, my Sallie, and please don't love me any the less. You cannot understand the *entente cordiale* between us 'old fellows.'

Faithfully,

Your

Soldier

Mechanicsville Turnpike, June 1, 1862

V

Concerning General Pickett's Presentiment of Danger the Night before he was Wounded at Gaines's Mill

ALL last night, my darling Sallie, the spirit of my dear mother seemed to hover over me. When she was living, and I used to feel in that way, I always, as sure as fate, received from her a letter written at the very time that I had the sensation of her presence. I wonder if up there she is watching over me, trying to send me some message — some warning. I wish I knew.

This morning my brigade moved from its canton' ments on the Williamsburg road and, by daybreak, was marching along the Mechanicsville turnpike, leading north of Richmond. The destination and char' acter of the expedition is unknown ; but the position of other troops indicates a general movement. This evening we crossed the Chickahominy and are biv' ouacked on our guns in the road in front of Mechan' icsville, from which point I am blessing my spirit and refreshing my soul by sending a message to my pro' mised wife. I am tired and sleepy, several times to' day going to sleep on my horse.

Before Gaines's Mill

This war was really never contemplated in earnest. I believe if either the North or the South had expected that their differences would result in this obstinate struggle, the cold-blooded Puritan and the cock hatted Huguenot and Cavalier would have made a compromise. Poor old Virginia came oftener than Noah's dove with her olive branch and though she desired to be loyal to the Union of States she did not believe in the right of coercion, and when called upon to furnish troops to restrain her sister states she refused, and would not even permit the passage of an armed force through her domain for that purpose. With no thought of cost, no consideration of disparity of relative strength or conditions, she rolled up her sleeves, ready to risk all in defense of a principle consecrated by the blood of her fathers. And now, alas, it is too late. We must carry through this bitter task unto the end. May the end be soon!

Your

Soldier

In Camp, June 27, 1862

VI

In which General Pickett, while Recovering from his Wound, Writes from his Old Home

IT is only when you are here with me, my darling, that I am not chafing, fretting, under my enforced absence from my command. As poor a marksman as the Yankee was who shot me, I wish he had been poorer still, aiming, as he must have been, either at my head or my heart and breaking my wing. He was frightened, too, I suspect, and had, besides, too much powder in his load. What did you want with that shot' smoked, burnt coat sleeve? The arm it held is yours, to work for you and shield you, my love, for always.

Impatient and restive as I am to get back to the field, letters and reports just received show me that I am not missed, and that my gallant old brigade is proving its valor as loyally under its new leader as when it so fearlessly followed your soldier. It held Waterloo Bridge against Pope while Jackson crossed the Rappahannock, and on the afternoon of the 30th received and repelled the onset of Fitz John Porter, magnificently clearing the field and winning a victory for our arms.

The news came, too, this morning of the death of

Kearny, one of the most brilliant generals of the Federal Army, a man whose fame as a soldier is world-wide. I knew him first in Mexico, where, as you know, he lost an arm at the siege of Mexico City. In Algeria he won the Cross of the Legion of Honor. He fought with the French in the battles of Magenta and Solferino and received also from Napoleon Third the decoration of the Legion of Honor. I wish we had taken him prisoner instead of shooting him. I hate to have such a man as Kearny killed. Marse Robert, who was his old friend, sent his body to Pope under a flag of truce. I am glad he did that — poor old Kearny!

The same courier brought the sad news that our Ewell had lost a leg and our Talliaferro had been wounded. And these are the horrors to which, when away from you, my beautiful darling, your soldier is impatient to return.

Never, never did men, since the world began, fight like ours! The Duke of Somerset, who sneeringly laughed when he saw our ragged, dirty, barefooted soldiers — "Mostly beardless boys," as he said — took off his hat in reverence when he saw them fight.

Lovingly,

Your

Soldier

July 15, 1862

VII

Mostly concerning Bob, General Pickett's ; Body-Servant

HOW I shall miss your visit to-day, my darling! I wish you had not gone. Don't stay. Doctor Minnegerode asked me this morning when he called, "Who sent the beautiful flowers?" Bob, to save me from answering, said, "De same young lady sont de flowers, Marse Doctor, dat 'broidered dat cape fer Marse George, en 'broidered dem dar slippers he's got on, en sont him de 'broidered stars dat he w'ars on his coat when he w'ars it; but *dat* young lady ain't de *onlyest* young lady dat sends Marse George flowers en things. Nor, Suh."

The dear old doctor understood; he winked at me and changed the subject. He is as loyal to the South, dear old fellow, as if his ancestors had landed at Jamestown. When he asked after my wound he said he would like to pray with me, though the dear old man pronounced it, with his German accent, 'bray.' And that reminded me of a story, and instead of hav' ing my thoughts and my heart set upon his beautiful prayer as I should have — miserable sinner that I was!

— I began thinking of Tom August, who said that one Sunday someone meeting him coming out of Old St. Paul's asked him what was the matter. He replied, "Oh, nothing. I'm not a jackass and I'm not going to bray, and old Doctor Minnegerode not only insists that I, but that his whole congregation, shall 'bray.' I, for one, will not do it and I don't want to make a row about it; so I came out. I wonder what the effect would be if we took him literally and did all 'bray'?"

Now, my darling, forgive this foolish story. I learned to like story-telling, listening as a boy to the best story-teller in the world, Mr. Lincoln.

Even the bird knows you are not coming to-day, for he doesn't sing. I shall hold you to the last line of your sweet note, which says, "I'll come to you, my soldier, before the flowers die." When Bob asked me, "Is Miss Sallie comin' dis ebenin' er in de mornin'?" I answered, "She does not mention any set time, Bob. She only says she'll come before the flowers die." "De flowers ain't waxinated flowers, is dey, Marse George?" he asked. "Den if dey ain't waxinated 'twon't be long fo' she is here."

When I asked him to hold the paper while I wrote, he humbly, beseechingly asked, "Please, Suh, Marse George, ef hit ain't axin' too much, when you comes cer writin' er dem dar words lak 'love' en 'honey' en 'darlin','' er any er dem poetry rhymes 'bout 'roses red en violets blue,' won't you please, Suh, show 'em ter me?" I didn't promise him, my sweetheart. I only said, "Hold that paper steady, Sir, and don't you let it slip." But when I did call you 'darling' or tell you I loved you, I felt so guilty that the rascal knew it, and grinned.

I mustn't write any more, my Sallie; but oh, I do love you—do love you forever and ever, and am

Your own

Soldier

July 18, 1862

VIII

Written upon General Pickett's Return to his Old Command

DARLING, my heart turns to you with a love so great that pain follows in its wake. You cannot understand this, my beautiful, bright-eyed, sunny-hearted princess? Your face is the sweetest face in all the world, mirroring, as it does, all that is pure and un-selfish, and I must not cast a shadow over it by the fears that come to me, in spite of myself. No, a sol-dier should not know fear of any kind. I must fight and plan and hope, and you must pray; pray for a real-ization of all our beautiful dreams, sitting beside our own hearthstone in our own home — you and I, you my goddess of devotion, and I your devoted slave. Words cannot express my devotion, though, my dar-ling, nor any known language my admiration and worship. At your feet your unworthy soldier bows in homage. All his soul, all his heart, yours now and for-ever. May God in his mercy spare his life and make it worthy of you!

My shoulder and arm are still quite stiff, and I can-not yet put my sleeve on the wounded arm. I have on one sleeve, and my coat is thrown over my other shoulder and arm. I can reach my mouth with my hand by bending my neck way over; so I am not help-less. Bob still buttons my collar, and does some other little services. Until I have more control of my arm, however, I shall confine myself to riding old Black, and not venture on Lucy. Enough of so small a matter.

My boys are delighted to welcome me back, show-ing their affection for me in many, many ways. Gar-nett is still in command of my dear old brigade, which was temporarily turned over to him when I was wounded and which, under his gallant leadership, has sustained its old reputation for fearlessness and endur-ance. I miss dear, familiar faces, for many of the brave fellows have been killed and wounded. You have heard me speak of Colonel Strange — a gallant soldier. He was wounded and left behind. After he was shot, the plucky old chap called out in a loud, clear voice, "Stand firm, boys; stand firm."

Well, the Yankees won the battle, but McClellan's delay in winning enabled Old Jack* to seize Harper's Ferry, so it was not so great a victory for them after all. Old Jack's note to Marse Robert, telling him of his success, was characteristic in both brevity and dic-

*General 'Stonewall' Jackson.

tion. He said, "Through God's mercy Harper's Ferry and its garrison are *to be* surrendered."

The seventeenth following is recorded in letters of blood for both armies, and in its wake came Lincoln's great political victory, proving the might of the pen, in his Emancipation Proclamation — winning with it the greatest victory yet for the North. It will behoove us now to heed well the old story of 'The Lark and the Husbandman', for it will be farewell to all foreign in tervention unless Greek meets Greek and we fight fire with fire and we, too, issue an Emancipation Procla mation. I pray God that the powers that reign will have the wisdom and foresight to see this in its true and all-pervading light. It would end the war, and I should assume as soon as practicable the rôle of school master and husband to the brightest little pupil and the sweetest little wife in all the world.

I'll write more later on. I've had many interrup tions and now I must stop. I don't want to, though. Oh, why do I love you so? Was ever sweetheart so loved before as my Sallie is loved by her own devoted

Soldier

P.S. Have been placed temporarily in command of a division.

Headquarters, Sept. 25, 1862

IX

Concerning General Jackson and General Garnett

MAY I hope, my precious, that when another year rolls by we can celebrate the anniversary of this day by announcing our marriage? To⁄day I was officially promoted to the rank of Major⁄General and permanently placed in command of a division. My dear old brigade, which I love and which was with me in the battles of Williamsburg, Seven Pines and Gaines's Mill, was assigned to Dick Garnett and there comes somehow, in spite of everything, a little 'kind of curious' feeling within when I hear it called 'Garnett's Brigade', even though he has been in command of it almost ever since I was wounded and has won for it distinction and from it love and respect.

Old Dick is a fine fellow, a brave, splendid soldier. He was in the Mexican war and was wounded in the battle of Mexico. He commanded a brigade under Old Jack, and was for a time in command of the fa⁄mous old 'Stonewall Brigade'. You have not met him, my sweetheart; but I want you to know him. His family are from Norfolk. He knows all your people, and remembers you as a child, and sends you his love.

26

GENERAL JACKSON AND GENERAL GARNETT

He is an old bachelor, though, and I don't know about sending this message — it is rather dangerous. No, no, my sweetheart, I am not afraid. I only wish, as I told old Dick, that he had a sweetheart just like you. He is as sensitive and proud as he is fearless and sweet-spirited, and has felt more keenly than most men would Old Jack's censure of him at the battle of Kernstown, when all his ammunition gave out and he withdrew his brigade from the field, for which he was arrested and relieved from duty. Old Jack told Lawton that in arresting Garnett he had no reference to his want of daring, which was surprising for Old Jack to say, who never explains anything.

Lawton, who is one of his generals, says Old Jack holds himself as the god of war, giving short, sharp commands, distinctly, rapidly and decisively, without consultation or explanation, and disregarding suggestions and remonstrances. Being himself absolutely fearless, and having unusual mental and moral, as well as physical, courage, he goes ahead on his own hook, asking no advice and resenting interference. He places no value on human life, caring for nothing so much as fighting, unless it be praying. Illness, wounds and all disabilities he defines as inefficiency and indications of a lack of patriotism. Suffering from insomnia, he often uses his men as a sedative, and when he can't sleep calls them up, marches them out a few miles; then marches them back. He never praises his men for gallantry, because it is their duty to be gallant and they do not deserve credit for doing their duty. Well, my own darling, I only pray that God may spare him to us to see us through. If General Lee had Grant's resources he would soon end the war; but Old Jack can do it without resources.

Bless your heart, here I am talking of these old war-horses to my prettice. Well, she knows how entirely I love her and how I have left in her keeping my soul's all.

Lovingly and faithfully, my Sallie, your own

Soldier

Headquarters, Oct. 11, 1862

X

From the Field of Fredericksburg

HERE we are, my darling, at Fredericksburg, on the south side of the Rappahannock, half-way between Richmond and Washington, fortified for us by the hand of the Great Father.

I penciled you a note by old Jackerie* on the 12th from the foot of the Hills between Hazel Run and the Telegraph Road. In it I sent a hyacinth, given me by a pretty lady who came out with beaten biscuit, and some unwritten and written messages from Old Peter and Old Jack, Hood, Ewell, Stuart and your 'brothers,' to the 'someone' to whom I was writing.

It seems an eternity, my Chulita, since the first of November when we moved on from Orange Court House. . . . I sent you a short note last night after the day's great battle, telling you that even in the midst of it all you were in my heart and thoughts.

My division, nine thousand strong, is in fine shape. It was on the field of battle, as a division, for the first time yesterday, though only one brigade, Kemper's, was actively engaged. What a day it was, my darling

*Headquarters Postmaster.

—this ever to be remembered by many of us thir-
teenth of December — dawning auspiciously upon
us, clad in deepest, darkest mourning. A fog such as
would shame London lay over the valley, and through
the dense mist *distinctly* came the uncanny commands
of the unseen opposing officers. My men were eager to
be in the midst of the fight, and if Hood had not been
so cautious they would probably have immortalized
themselves. Old Peter's orders were that Hood and
myself were to hold our ground of defense, unless we
should see an opportunity to attack the enemy while
engaged with A. P. Hill on the right. A little after
ten, when the fog had lifted, and Stuart's cannon from
the plain of Massaponax were turned upon Meade,
and when Franklin's advance left the enemy's flank
open, I went up to Hood and urged him to seize the
opportunity. But he was afraid to assume so great a
responsibility, and sent for permission to Old Peter,
who was with Marse Robert in a different part of the
field. Before his assent and approval were received,
the opportunity, alas, was lost.

If war, my own, is a necessity — and I suppose it
is—it is a very cruel one. Your soldier's heart almost
stood still as he watched those sons of Erin fearlessly
rush to their death. The brilliant assault on Marye's

Heights of their Irish Brigade was beyond description. Why, my darling, we forgot they were fighting us, and cheer after cheer at their fearlessness went up all along our lines. About fifty of my division sleep their last sleep at the foot of Marye's Heights.

I can't help feeling sorry for Old Burnside — proud, plucky, hard-headed old dog. I always liked him; but I loved little Mac,* and it was a godsend to the Confederacy that he was relieved.

Oh, my darling, war and its results did not seem so awful till the love for you came. Now — now I want to love and bless and help everything; and there are no foes — no enemies — just love for you and longing for you.

Your

Soldier

Fredericksburg, Dec. 14, 1862

---

* General McClellan.

XI

From General Pickett's Old Home, on the Suffolk Expedition

I RODE on ahead of my division, stopped for a moment at our old home, ran into the garden and gathered for my darling some lilies of the valley, planted by my sweet mother, which I knew were now in the full glory of their blossoming. As I plucked them one by one, I thought of the dear mother who had planted them and the sweet bride-to-be who would receive them, and my heart went up in gratitude for the great love given me by both sweetheart and mother.

While I am writing to you, Braxton, and the cook, and the whole household, in fact, are busy getting a lunch for me and preparing to load up my courier and my boy, Bob, with as many more lunches as they can carry, to be distributed as far as they will go. My little sister is making a paper box to hold my lilies for you, and I am writing a love-letter to stand sentinel over them and guard the sweet, sacred messages entrusted to them. Old Jackerie will take them to you, and will also bring you, with my sister's love, a box of her own home/made dulces.

Perhaps, sweetheart, *perhaps* I say, you will see your soldier sooner than you think. You know that since the capture of Roanoke Island and our abandonment of Norfolk and Suffolk, all that section of the country has been in the hands of the enemy. Now, in the ex/treme northeast corner of North Carolina are stored away large quantities of corn and bacon. Old Peter, our far/seeing, slow but sure, indefatigable, plodding old war/horse, has planned to secure some of these sorely needed supplies for our poor, half fed army — and there never was such an army, such an uncom/plaining, plucky body of men — never!

Why, my Sallie, during these continuous ten days' march, the ground snowy and sleety, the feet of many of the soldiers covered only with improvised moc/casins of raw beef hide, and hundreds of them with/out shoes or blankets or overcoats, they have not uttered one word of complaint. No, nor one murmur/ing tone; but cheerily, singing or telling stories, they have tramped — tramped — tramped. To crown it all, after having marched sixty miles over half frozen, slushy roads they passed to/day through Richmond, the home of many of them, without a halt, with not a straggler—greeted and cheered by sweethearts, wives, mothers and friends. "God bless you, my darling," "God bless you, my son," "Hello, old man," "Howdy, Charley," rang all along the line. Lunches, slices of bread and meat, bottles of milk or hot coffee, were thrust into grateful hands by the dear people of Richmond, who thus brought comfort and cheer to many a hungry one besides their very own, as the men hurriedly returned the greetings and marched on. You would hardly recognize these ragged, barefooted soldiers as the trim, tidy boys of two years ago, in their handsome gray uniforms, with shining equipment and full haversacks and knapsacks.

Be brave and help me to be brave, my darling, and to trust in God. I won't say, 'Keep your powder dry', for one who doesn't know enough to do that is not much of a soldier.

Faithfully and lovingly and forever your own

Soldier

Richmond, February —, 1863

XII

In which General Pickett Urges his Betrothed to Marry him at once

THIS morning I awakened from a beautiful dream, and while its glory still overshadows the waking and fills my soul with radiance I write to make an earnest request — entreating, praying, that you will grant it. You know, my sweetheart, we have no prophets in these days to tell us how near or how far is the end of this awful struggle. If the battle is not to the strong, then we may win; but when all our ports are closed and the world is against us, when for us a man killed is a man lost, while Grant may have twenty-five of every nation to replace one of his, it seems that the battle is to the strong. So often already has hope been dashed to the winds.

Why, only a little while since, the Army of the Potomac recrossed the Rappahannock, defeated, broken in spirit, the men deserting, the subordinate officers so severe in their criticism of their superiors that the great Commander-in-Chief of the Army, Mr. Lin-

coln, felt it incumbent upon him to write a severe let/
ter of censure and rebuke. Note the change, and hear
their bugle/call of hope. Hooker, who is alleged to
have 'the finest army on the planet', is reported to be
on the eve of moving against Richmond. My division
and that of Hood, together with the artillery of Dear/
ing and Henry, have been ordered to a point near
Petersburg to meet this possible movement.

Now, my Sallie, may angels guide my pen and help
me to write — help me to voice this longing desire
of my heart and to intercede for me with you for a
speedy fulfillment of your promise to be my wife. As
you know, it is imperative that I should remain at my
post and absolutely impossible for me to come for you.
So you will have to come to me. Will you, dear? Will
you come? Can't your beautiful eyes see beyond the
mist of my eagerness and anxiety that in the bewil/
derment of my worship — worshiping, as I do, one so
divinely right, and feeling that my love is returned —
how hard it is for me to ask you to overlook old/time
customs, remembering only that you are to be a sol/
dier's wife? A week, a day, an hour, as your husband,
would engulf in its great joy all my past woes and
ameliorate all future fears.

So, my precious one, don't delay; send me a line

back by Jackerie saying you will come. Come at once, my own, into this valley of the shadow of uncertainty, and make certain the comfort that if I should fall I shall fall as your husband.

You know that I love you with a devotion that envelops, absorbs, all else — a devotion so divine that when in dreams I see you it is as something too pure and sacred for mortal touch. And if you only knew the heavenly life which thrills me through when I make it real to myself that you love me, you would understand. Think, my dear little one, of the uncertainty and dangers of even a day of separation, and don't let the time come when either of us will look back and say, "It might have been."

If I am spared, my precious, all my life shall be devoted to making you happy, to keeping all that might hurt you far from you, to making all that is good come near to you. Heaven will help me to be ever helpful to you, and will bless me to bless you. If you knew how every hour I kneel at your altar, if you could hear the prayers I offer to you and to our Heavenly Father for you, if you knew the incessant thought and longing and desire to make you blessed, you would know how much your answer will mean to me and how, while I plead, I am held back by a reverence and a sensitive adoration for you. For, my Sallie, you are my goddess, and I am only

> Your devoted,
>
> Soldier

In Camp, April 15, 1863

XIII

Concerning an Anticipated Skirmish

HOPING, praying, yes and believing, my precious one, that you heeded your soldier's admonition, and are now safe across the "Black Water", I am tak⁄ing the risk of sending to you at Ivor, by my boy, Bob, a little box of dulces and a note filled with adoration. I hope that both will reach you safely, and that Bob will return with good news.

My orders to follow Hood's Division have been countermanded. Hood was hurried on from the "Black Water" by rail to rejoin Marse Robert, who has just gained a great victory at Chancellorsville. I am ordered instead to proceed *at once* with three of my brigades to Petersburg, via the "Jerusalem⁄Plank⁄Road", to intercept a cavalry raid reported to be com⁄ing down the south side of the James River.

Perhaps, my Sallie, I shall have met these raiders ere this reaches you. Who knows how many of us may then hear the roll⁄call from the other side and be sorry? But sorry for whom? For the comrades who answer to their names and are reported present, or for those whose spirit voices, just born, have not yet

39

gained the power to reach the ear of the orderly and who are reported dead, even though they, too, answer, "Here"? For, my darling, *there is no death*, and you must feel — must *know* — now and always, that whether here or there, at the roll-call your soldier answers, "*Here*".

Now, *a Dios*, my beloved. Close your brown eyes and feel my arms around you, for I am holding you close — oh, so close.

Forever your own loving

Soldier

Suffolk, May 5, 1863

XIV

General Lee Crosses the Potomac

EACH day, my darling, takes me farther and farther away from you, from all I love and hold
dear. We have been guarding the passes of the Blue
Ridge. To-day, under orders from Marse Robert, we
cross the Potomac. McLaws' and Hood's Divisions,
and the three brigades of my division, follow on after
Hill. May our Heavenly Father bless us with an early
and a victorious return. But even then, the price of
it — the price of it, my little one — the blood of our
countrymen. God in His mercy temper the wind to
us.

As I returned the salute of my men, many of them
beardless boys, the terrible responsibility as their
Commander almost overwhelmed me, and my heart
was rent in prayer for guidance and help. Oh, the
desolate homes, the widows, the orphans, and the
heart-broken mothers, that this campaign will make!
How many of them, my men, so full of hope and
cheer now, will cross that other river which will
bring them to the Eternal Home.

Have faith, my little one, and keep up a brave

heart. Your soldier feels that he will return to claim his bride—his beautiful bride. And then we will be so happy, my darling; and all our days to come, we will show our loving gratitude to our Father for His mercy in sparing us to each other.

Now, *vida de mi alma*, my Sallie—how I hate to say it—*a Dios*. Do you remember how many times we said good-by that last evening? And then as I heard the latch of the gate click and shut me outside, I was obliged to go back. I could not stand the cruelty of the sound of that latch — it seemed to knife my soul. I turned back. The door was open; I came in. You thought I had gone. I can't just remember how many times I said good night. I know I did not close the gate as I went out again. Keep another gate open for the good morning, my precious bride-to-be. Oh, the bliss to be—the bliss to be then for —

Your
Soldier

In Camp, June 18, 1863

XV

On the Way through Pennsylvania

I NEVER could quite enjoy being a "Conquering Hero". No, my Sallie, there is something radically wrong about my Hurrahism. I can fight for a cause I know to be just, can risk my own life and the lives of those in my keeping without a thought of the consequences; but when we've conquered, when we've downed the enemy and won the victory, I don't want to hurrah. I want to go off all by myself and be sorry for them — want to lie down in the grass, away off in the woods somewhere or in some lone valley on the hillside far from all *human* sound, and rest my soul and put my heart to sleep and get back something — I don't know what — but something I had that is gone from me — something subtle and unexplainable — something I never knew I possessed till I had lost it — till it was gone — gone.

Yesterday my men were marching victoriously through the little town of Greencastle, the bands all playing our glorious, soul inspiring, Southern airs: 'The Bonny Blue Flag', 'My Maryland', 'Her Bright Smile Haunts Me Still', and the soldiers all happy, hopeful, joyously keeping time to the music, many

43

following it with their voices, and making up for the want of the welcome they were receiving in the enemy's country by cheering themselves and giving themselves a welcome. As Floweree's band, playing 'Dixie', was passing a vine-bowered home, a young girl rushed out on the porch and waved a United States flag. Then, either fearing that it might be taken from her or finding it too large and unwieldy, she fastened it around her as an apron, and taking hold of it on each side, and waving it in defiance, called out with all the strength of her girlish voice and all the courage of her brave young heart:

"Traitors—traitors—traitors, come and take this flag, the man of you who dares!"

Knowing that many of my men were from a section of the country which had been within the enemy's lines, and fearing lest some might forget their manhood, I took off my hat and bowed to her, saluted her flag and then turned, facing the men who felt and saw my unspoken order. And don't you know that they were all Virginians and didn't forget it, and that almost every man lifted his cap and cheered the little maiden who, though she kept on waving her flag, ceased calling us traitors, till, finally, letting it drop in front of her, she cried out:

44

ON THE WAY THROUGH PENNSYLVANIA

"Oh, I wish — I wish I had a rebel flag — I'd wave that, too!"

The picture of that little girl in the vine-covered porch, beneath the purple morning glories with their closed lips and bowed heads waiting and saving their prettiness and bloom for the coming morn—of course, I thought of *you*, my beautiful darling. For the time, that little Greencastle Yankee girl with her belovèd flag was my own little promised-to-be-wife, my Sallie, receiving from her soldier and her soldier's soldiers the reverence and homage due her.

We left the little girl standing there with the flag gathered up in her arms, as if too sacred to be waved, now that even the enemy had done it reverence.

Forever your devoted

Soldier

Greencastle, Pa., June 24, 1863

XVI

On the Road to Gettysburg

WE crossed the Potomac on the 24th at Williamsport and went into bivouac on the Maryland side, from which place I sent my Lady-Love a long letter and some flowers gathered on the way. We then went on to Hagerstown, where we met A. P. Hill's Corps, which had crossed the river farther down. From Hagerstown I sent to the same and only Lady-Love another letter, which was not only freighted with all the adoration and devotion of her soldier's heart, but contained messages from the staff and promises to take care of him and bring him safely back to her.

We made no delay at Hagerstown but, passing through in the rear of Hill's Corps, moved on up the Cumberland Valley and bivouacked at Greencastle, where the most homesick letter of all yet written was sent to — well, guess *whom* this time. Why, to the same Lady-Love, the sweetest, loveliest flower that ever blossomed to bless and make fairer a beautiful world — for it is beautiful, betokening in its loveliness nothing of wickedness or woe — nothing of this deadly strife between men who should be brethren of a great and common cause, as they are the inheritors of a great and common country.

The officers and men are all in excellent condition, bright and cheerful, singing songs and telling stories, full of hope and courage, inspired with absolute faith and confidence in our success. There is no straggling, no disorder, no dissatisfaction, no plundering, and there are no desertions. Think of it — an army of sixty thousand men marching through the enemy's country without the *least* opposition. The object of this great movement is, of course, unknown to us. Its purpose, and our destination, are known at present only to the Commanding General and his Chief Lieutenants. The officers and men generally believe that the intention is entirely to surround the Army of the Potomac and to place Washington and Baltimore within our grasp. They think that Marse Robert is merely threatening the Northern cities, with the view of suddenly turning down the Susquehanna, cutting off all railroad connections, destroying all bridges, throwing his army north of Baltimore and cutting off Washington, and that Beauregard is to follow on directly from Richmond via Manassas to Washington, in rear of Hooker, who of course will be in pursuit of Marse Robert.

Nous verrons.

We reached here this morning, June 27th, the anniversary of the battle of Gaines's Mill, where your soldier was wounded. We marched straight through the town of Chambersburg, which was more deserted than Goldsmith's village. The stores and houses were all closed, with here and there groups of uncheerful Boers of Deutschland descent, earnestly talking, more sylvan shadows than smiles wreathing their faces. I had given orders that the bands were not to play; but as we were marching through the northeastern part of the city, some young ladies came out onto the veranda of one of the prettiest homes in the town and asked:

"Would you mind shooting off the bands a bit?"

So the command was given, and the band played 'Home Sweet Home', 'Annie Laurie', 'Her Bright Smile Haunts Me Still', 'Nellie Gray', and 'Hazel Dell.' The young ladies asked the next band that passed if they wouldn't play 'Dixie'. But the band instead struck up 'The Old Oaken Bucket', 'The Swanee River', 'The Old Arm Chair', 'The Lone Rock by the Sea', and 'Auld Lang Syne'.

"Thought you was rebels. Where'd you come from anyhow? Can't play 'Dixie', none of you?" they

48

called out. We marched straight on through the city, and are camped four miles beyond the town, on the York River road.

To-morrow, if you'll promise not to divulge it to a human soul, I'll tell you a great secret. No, my Sallie, I can't wait till to-morrow. I'll tell you right now. So listen and cross your heart that you won't tell. I love you — love you — love you, and oh, little one, I want to see you so. That is the secret.

A Dios. With my heart at your feet, and my hap-piness in your hands, I am,

Lovingly and forever,

Your

Soldier

Chambersburg, June 27, 1863

XVII

During a Halt in the March

I WISH, my Sallie, you could see this wonderfully
rich and prosperous country, abounding in plenty,
with its great, strong, vigorous horses and oxen, its
cows and crops and verdantly thriving vegetation —
none of the ravages of war, no signs of devastation —
all in woeful contrast to the land where we lay dream⁄
ing. All the time I break the law 'Thou shalt not
covet', for every fine horse or cow I see I want for
my darling, and all the pretty things I see besides.
Never mind, she shall have everything some day,
and I shall have the universe and heaven's choicest
gift when she is my wife — all my very own.

At Chambersburg, Marse Robert preached us a
sermon, first instructing us in the meaning of 'meum'
and 'teum', and then taking as his text, 'Vengeance
is Mine, saith the Lord'. I observed that the mourn⁄
ers' bench was not overcrowded with seekers for con⁄
version. The poor fellows were thinking of their own
despoiled homes, looted of everything, and were not
wildly enthusiastic as they obediently acquiesced to
our beloved Commander's order. The Yanks have

taken into the mountains and across the Susquehanna all the supplies they could, and we pay liberally for those which we are compelled to take, giving them money which is paid to us, our own Confederate script. Some of us have a few pieces of gold with which to purchase some keepsake or token for the dear ones at home. Alas, my little one, how many of us will be blessed with the giving of them? God in His mercy be our Commander-in-Chief.

We have not a wide field for selection here, as we once had at Price's dry goods store or John Tyler's jewelry establishment in Richmond; but it seems quite magnificent to us now, since the Richmond counters are so bare as to offer not even a wedding ring or a yard of calico. We are guying General C—— who, after long and grave deliberation, bought three hoop skirts as a present for his betrothed.

All that makes life dear is the thought of seeing you and being with you. And oh, what an eternity it seems since I said good night. Oh, my darling, love me, pray for me, hold me in your thoughts, keep me in your heart.

Our whole army is now in Pennsylvania, north of the river. There were rumors that Richmond was threatened from all sides — Dix from Old Point,

Getty from Hanover, Keyes from Bottom's Bridge, and so on — and that we might be recalled. It turned out to be Munchausen, and we are still to march for-ward. Every tramp — tramp — tramp is a thought — thought — thought of my darling, every halt a blessing invoked, every command a loving caress; and the thought of you and prayer for you make me strong, make me better, give me courage, give me faith. Now, my dearest, let my soul speak to yours. Listen — listen — listen — You hear — I am an-swered.

Forever and ever,

Your

Soldier

In Camp, June 29, 1863

XVIII

While General Pickett Awaited the Order to Charge at Gettysburg

CAN my prettice do patchwork? If she can, she must piece together these penciled scraps of soiled paper and make out of them, not a log-cabin quilt, but a wren's nest, cement it with love and fill it with blue and golden and speckled eggs of faith and hope, to hatch out greater love yet for us.

Well, Sallie mine, the long, wearying march from Chambersburg, through dust and heat beyond compare, brought us here yesterday (a few miles from Gettysburg). Though my poor men were almost exhausted by the march in the intense heat, I felt that the exigencies demanded my assuring Marse Robert that we had arrived and that, with a few hours' rest, my men would be equal to anything he might require of them. I sent Walter with my message and rode on myself to Little Round Top to see Old Peter, who, I tell you, was mighty glad to see me. And now, just think of it, though the old war-horse was watching A. P. Hill's attack upon the center and Hood and McLaws of his own corps, who had struck Sickles, he turned, and before referring to the fighting or asking about the march, inquired after *you*, my darling. While we were watching the fight, Walter came back with Marse Robert's reply to my message, which was in part: "Tell Pickett I'm glad that he has come, that I can always depend upon him and his men, but that I shall not want him this evening."

We have been on the *qui vive*, my Sallie, since midnight; and as early as three o'clock were on the march. About half past three, Gary's pistol signaled the Yankees' attack upon Culp's Hill, and with its echo a wail of regret went up from my very soul that the other two brigades of my old division had been left behind. Oh, God! — if only I had them! — a surety for the honor of Virginia, for I can depend upon them, little one. They know your soldier and would follow him into the very jaws of death, and he will need them — right there, too, before he's through.

At early dawn, darkened by the threatening rain, Armistead, Garnett, Kemper and your soldier held a heart-to-heart powwow.

All three sent regards to you, and Old Lewis pulled

a ring from his little finger and, making me take it, said, "Give this little token, George, please, to her of the sunset eyes, with my love, and tell her the 'old man' says since he could not be the lucky dog he's mighty glad that you are."

Dear old Lewis—dear old 'Lo', as Magruder always called him, being short for Lothario. Well, my Sallie, I'll keep the ring for you, and some day I'll take it to John Tyler and have it made into a breast' pin and set around with rubies and diamonds and emeralds. You will be the pearl, the other jewel. Dear old Lewis!

Just as we three separated to go our different ways after silently clasping hands, our fears and prayers voiced in the "Good luck, old man," a summons came from Old Peter, and I immediately rode to the top of the ridge where he and Marse Robert were making a reconnaissance of Meade's position. "Great God!" said Old Peter as I came up. "Look, General Lee, at the insurmountable difficulties between our line and that of the Yankees—the steep hills—the tiers of artillery—the fences—the heavy skirmish line— And then we'll have to fight our infantry against their batteries. Look at the ground we'll have to charge over, nearly a mile of that open ground there under the rain of their canister and shrapnel."

"The enemy is there, General Longstreet, and I am going to strike him," said Marse Robert in his firm, quiet, determined voice.

About 8 o'clock I rode with them along our line of prostrate infantry. They had been told to lie down to prevent attracting attention, and though they had been forbidden to cheer they voluntarily arose and lifted in reverential adoration their caps to our beloved commander as we rode slowly along. Oh, the responsibility for the lives of such men as these! Well, my darling, their fate and that of our beloved Southland will be settled ere your glorious brown eyes rest on these scraps of penciled paper—your soldier's last letter, perhaps.

Our line of battle faces Cemetery Ridge. Our detachments have been thrown forward to support our artillery which stretches over a mile along the crests of Oak Ridge and Seminary Ridge. The men are lying in the rear, my darling, and the hot July sun pours its scorching rays almost vertically down upon them. The suffering and waiting are almost unbearable.

.   .   .   .

Well, my sweetheart, at one o'clock the awful si/lence was broken by a cannon/shot, and then another, and then more than a hundred guns shook the hills from crest to base, answered by more than another hundred — the whole world a blazing volcano — the whole of heaven a thunderbolt — then darkness and absolute silence — then the grim and gruesome, low/spoken commands — then the forming of the attack/ing columns. My brave Virginians are to attack in front. Oh, God in mercy help me as He never helped before!

I have ridden up to report to Old Peter. I shall give him this letter to mail to you and a package to give you if — Oh, my darling, do you feel the love of my heart, the prayer, as I write that fatal word 'if'?

Old Peter laid his hand over mine and said: — "I know, George, I know — but I can't do it, boy. Alexander has my instructions. He will give you the order." There was silence, and his hand still rested on

57

mine when a courier rode up and handed me a note from Alexander.

Now, I go; but remember always that I love you with all my heart and soul, with every fiber of my being; that now and forever I am yours — yours, my beloved. It is almost three o'clock. My soul reaches out to yours — my prayers. I'll keep up a brave heart for Virginia and for you, my darling.

Your
Soldier

Gettysburg, July 3, 1863

XIX

Relating Certain Incidents of the Battle

MY letter of yesterday, my darling, written before the battle, was full of hope and cheer; even though it told you of the long hours of waiting from four in the morning, when Gary's pistol rang out from the Federal lines signaling the attack upon Culp's Hill, to the solemn eight o'clock review of my men, who rose and stood silently lifting their hats in loving reverence as Marse Robert, Old Peter and your own soldier reviewed them — on then to the deadly stillness of the five hours following, when the men lay in the tall grass in the rear of the artillery line, the July sun pouring its scorching rays almost vertically down upon them, till one o'clock when the awful silence of the vast battlefield was broken by a cannonshot which opened the greatest artillery duel of the world. The firing lasted two hours. When it ceased we took advantage of the blackened field and in the glowering darkness formed our attacking column just before the brow of Seminary Ridge.

I closed my letter to you a little before three o'clock and rode up to Old Peter for orders. I found him like a great lion at bay. I have never seen him so grave and troubled. For several minutes after I had saluted him he looked at me without speaking. Then in an agonized voice, the reserve all gone, he said:

"Pickett, I am being crucified at the thought of the sacrifice of life which this attack will make. I have instructed Alexander to watch the effect of our fire upon the enemy, and when it begins to tell he must take the responsibility and give you your orders, for I can't."

While he was yet speaking a note was brought to me from Alexander. After reading it I handed it to him, asking if I should obey and go forward. He looked at me for a moment, then held out his hand. Presently, clasping his other hand over mine without speaking he bowed his head upon his breast. I shall never forget the look in his face nor the clasp of his hand when I said: — "Then, General, I shall lead my Division on." I had ridden only a few paces when I remembered your letter and (forgive me) thought-lessly scribbled in a corner of the envelope, "If Old Peter's nod means death then good-by and God bless you, little one," turned back and asked the dear old chief if he would be good enough to mail it for me. As he took your letter from me, my darling, I saw tears glistening on his cheeks and beard. The stern old war-horse, God bless him, was weeping for his men and, I know, praying too that this cup might pass from them. I obeyed the silent assent of his bowed head, an assent given against his own convictions, — given in anguish and with reluctance.

My brave boys were full of hope and confident of victory as I led them forth, forming them in column of attack, and though officers and men alike knew what was before them, — knew the odds against them, — they eagerly offered up their lives on the altar of duty, having absolute faith in their ultimate success. Over on Cemetery Ridge the Federals beheld a scene never before witnessed on this continent, — a scene which has never previously been enacted and can never take place again — an army forming in line of battle in full view, under their very eyes — charging across a space nearly a mile in length over fields of waving grain and anon of stubble and then a smooth expanse — moving with the steadiness of a dress parade, the pride and glory soon to be crushed by an overwhelming heartbreak.*

.   .   .   .

* General Pickett, in his first official report to General Lee, pointed out without reserve the circumstances he deemed re-

GENERAL PICKETT'S LETTERS

Well, it is all over now. The battle is lost, and many of us are prisoners, many are dead, many wounded, bleeding and dying. Your soldier lives and mourns and but for you, my darling, he would rather, a million times rather, be back there with his dead, to sleep for all time in an unknown grave.

Your sorrowing

Soldier

In Camp, July 4, 1863

---

sponsible for the disastrous result of his charge. General Lee, 'to guard against dissensions', requested General Pickett to destroy both copy and original of his report, substituting another in its place. This was done.

At this point in the above letter follows an account of the battle embodying, according to the statement of Mrs. Pickett, material similar to General Pickett's report to General Lee. Mrs. Pickett feels that this portion of the letter should be withheld from publication. It has been accordingly omitted — A. C. I.

XX

Written in Sorrow and Defeat

ON the Fourth — far from a glorious Fourth to us or to any with love for his fellow-men — I wrote you just a line of heart-break. The sacrifice of life on that blood-soaked field on the fatal third was too awful for the heralding of victory, even for our victorious foe, who, I think, believe as we do, that it decided the fate of our cause. No words can picture the anguish of that roll-call — the breathless waits between the responses. The "Here" of those who, by God's mercy, had miraculously escaped the awful rain of shot and shell was a sob — a gasp — a knell — for the unanswered name of his comrade called before his. There was no tone of thankfulness for having been spared to answer to their names, but rather a toll, and an unvoiced wish that they, too, had been among the missing.

But for the blight to your sweet young life, but for you, only you, my darling, your soldier would rather by far be out there, too, with his brave Virginians — dead —

Even now I can hear them cheering as I gave the

order, "Forward"! I can feel their faith and trust in me and their love for our cause. I can feel the thrill of their joyous voices as they called out all along the line, "We'll follow you, Marse George. We'll follow you — we'll follow you." Oh, how faithfully they kept their word — following me on — on — to their death, and I, believing in the promised support, led them on — on — on — Oh, God!

I can't write you a love letter to-day, my Sallie, for with my great love for you and my gratitude to God for sparing my life to devote to you, comes the overpowering thought of those whose lives were sacrificed — of the broken-hearted widows and mothers and orphans. The moans of my wounded boys, the sight of the dead, upturned faces, flood my soul with grief — and here am I whom they trusted, whom they followed, leaving them on that field of carnage — leaving them to the mercy of —— and guarding four thousand prisoners across the river back to Winchester. Such a duty for men who a few hours ago covered themselves with glory eternal.

Well, my darling, I put the prisoners all on their honor and gave them equal liberties with my own soldier boys. My first command to them was to go and enjoy themselves the best they could, and they have obeyed my order. To-day a Dutchman and two of his comrades came up and told me that they were lost and besought me to help them find their commands. They had been with my men and had gotten separated from their own comrades. So I sent old Floyd off on St. Paul to find out where they belonged and deliver them.

This is too gloomy and too poor a letter for so beau-tiful a sweetheart, but it seems sacrilegious, almost, to say I love you, with the hearts that are stilled to love on the field of battle.

Your

Soldier

Headquarters, July 6, 1863

XXI

In which General Pickett Recrosses the Potomac

I HAVE but one moment to tell my own darling how entirely my heart is hers. But for her and her love, I should not have cared to survive the conflict of the 3rd. My division is almost extinguished. How any of us escaped is miraculous. More than a fourth of my division have been placed *hors du combat*. Two of my brigadiers were killed, and one wounded and a prisoner. Only two field officers out of the whole command came out of the fight unhurt.

I was ordered to take a height, which I did, under the most withering fire I have ever known, and I have seen many battles. But, alas, *no support came;* and my poor fellows who had gotten in were over⁄powered. My heart is very, very sad!

I am crossing the river to⁄day, guarding some four thousand prisoners back to Winchester, where I shall take command and recruit my wearied and cut up people.

You must write to me at that place. I received a letter from you dated the fourteenth of last month, immediately after you arrived at your home. I was

delighted to learn of your mother's convalescence.
Give her my best love, and tell her to take good care
of my own, own precious.

Devotedly and forever,

Your

Soldier

Just one month to⁄day since I parted from you
it seems a year.

Williamsport, July 8, 1863

XXII

Containing Further Details of the Battle

I AM enclosing you a copy of General Lee's official letter of July 9th, in answer to mine of the 8th, the same day on which I wrote you (who deserved something brighter) that ghostly, woeful letter.

General Lee's letter has been published to the division in general orders, and has been received with appreciative satisfaction — for the soldiers, one and all, love and honor Lee, and his sympathy and praise are always very dear to them. Just after the order was published I heard one of the men, rather rough and uncouth and not, as are most of the men, to the manner born, say, as he wiped away the tears with the back of his hand : " Dag'gone him, dag'gone him, dag'gone his old soul, I'm blamed ef I wouldn't be dag'gone willin' to go right through it all and be killed again with them others to hear Marse Robert, dag'gone him, say over again as how he grieved bout'n we'all's losses and honored us for we'all's bravery! Darned ef I wouldn't!" Isn't that reverential adora'tion, my darling, to be willing to be 'killed again' for a word of praise ?

Further Details of the Battle

It seems selfish and inhuman to speak of love — haunted as I am with the unnecessary sacrifice of the lives of so many of my brave boys. I can't think of anything but the desolate homes in Virginia and the unknown dead in Pennsylvania. At the beginning of the fight I was so sanguine, so sure of success! Early in the morning I had been assured by Alexander that General Lee had ordered that every brigade in his command was to charge Cemetery Hill; so I had no fear of not being supported. Alexander also assured me of the support of his artillery, which would move ahead of my division in the advance. He told me that he had borrowed seven twelve-pound howitzers from Pendleton, Lee's Chief of Artillery, which he had put in reserve to accompany me.

In the morning I rode with him while he, by Longstreet's orders, selected the salient angle of the wood in which my line was formed, which line was just on the left of his seventy-five guns. At about a quarter to three o'clock, when his written order to make the charge was handed to me, and dear Old Peter after reading it in sorrow and fear reluctantly bowed his head in assent, I obeyed, leading my three brigades straight on the enemy's front, Kemper and Garnett in front and Armistead on Garnett's left. You never saw anything like it. They moved across that field of death as a battalion marches forward in line of battle upon drill, each commander in front of his command leading and cheering on his men. Two lines of the enemy's infantry were driven back; two lines of guns were taken — and no support came. Pendleton, without Alexander's knowledge, had sent four of the guns which he had loaned him to some other part of the field, and the other three guns could not be found. The two brigades which were to have followed me had, poor fellows, been seriously engaged in the fights of the two previous days. Both of their commanding officers had been killed, and while they had been replaced by gallant, competent officers, these new leaders were unknown to the men.

Ah, if I had only had my other two brigades, a different story would have been flashed to the world. It was too late to retreat; and to go on was death or capture. Poor old Dick Garnett did not dismount, as did the others of us, and he was killed instantly, falling from his horse. Kemper was desperately wounded; was brought from the field but was subsequently taken prisoner. Dear old Lewis Armistead, God bless him, was mortally wounded at the head of his command, after planting the flag of Virginia within the enemy's lines. Seven of my colonels, Hodges, Edmonds, Magruder, Williams, Patten, Allen, and Owens, were killed; and one, Stuart, was mortally wounded. Nine of my lieutenant colonels, Carrington, Otey, Richardson, Hunton, Terry, Garnett, Mayo, Phillips, and Aylett, were wounded; and three, Colcott, Wade, and Ellis, were killed. Only one field officer of my whole command, Colonel Cabell, was unhurt; and the loss of my company officers was in proportion.

I wonder, my dear, if in the light of the Great Eternity we shall any of us feel this was for the best and shall have learned to say, "Thy will be done."

No castles today, sweetheart. No, the bricks of happiness and the mortar of love must lie untouched in this lowering gloom. Pray, dear, for the sorrowing ones —

Faithfully and lovingly and forever,

Your

Soldier

Headquarters, July —, 1863

Headquarters, A. N. Va.,
July 9th, 1863.

General:

Your letter of the 8th has been received. It was with reluctance that I imposed upon your gallant division the duty of carrying prisoners to Staunton. I regretted to assign them to such a service, as well as to separate them from the Army, though temporarily, with which they have been so long and efficiently associated. Though small in numbers, their worth is not diminished, and I had supposed that the division itself would be loth to part from its comrades, at a time when the presence of every man is so essential.

No one grieves more than I do at the loss suffered by your noble division in the recent conflict, or honors it more for its bravery and gallantry. It will afford me hereafter satisfaction, when an opportunity occurs, to do all in my power to recruit its diminished ranks, and to recognize it in the most efficient manner.

Very respectfully, your obedient servant,

R. E. LEE, General.

Major Gen. G. E. Pickett, commanding,
   Forwarded through Lieut. Gen. Longstreet.
    C. MARSHALL, Major and A. D. C.

XXIII

On the Way to Richmond

IT would be impossible, my darling, to describe to you even the half of the horrors and hard/ ships of these last days, from the first night's long march to the present hour; not only for ourselves but for the prisoners whom, with shattered hopes and heartbreak we, the little remnant of my division, have been assigned to guard. "One prisoner is too many for us, who haven't a crust to go around among our/ selves," as Old Jack said.

Your sensitive, poetic nature, my darling, will, I know, rebel with mine at this humiliating position of provost/guard. Oh, the pity of it, guarding these prisoners through their own country, depleted and suffering mentally and physically as we are, and be/ ing forced to march forward with a speed beyond their own and our endurance! It may be some con/ solation to both that we suffer alike from fatigue, hunger, exhaustion and wet — for the excessive rains which set in on the fourth have continued unabated.

The long wagon/trains, the artillery, the assort/ ment of vehicles of all kinds impressed from the farmers and loaded to their utmost capacity with our wounded and, anon, room made for the crowding in of yet another, falling from illness or exhaustion all along our way, have added their quota to the discom' forts of the march. Our commissariat, too, has been as wretched here in this land of plenty as it was in the barren, war'ridden land we left behind. Our banquets, we, the guard of honor, and our guests, the prisoners, have shared like'and'like, and none was ever more enjoyed by either than the flour made into paste and baked on the stones in front of the fire, and the good Pennsylvania beef roasted on the end of a stick. By the way, my Sallie, when you are my little housekeeper, you must remember that this stick'end roasting is a mighty toothsome recipe for cooking beef.

The prisoners have been far more cheerful than we have been, for they have not only had strong hope of being retaken by their own arms within a few days, but their army has gained a great victory, and though dearly bought, it has, I fear, decided the fate of our new'born nation. The cannonading on the second morning, the shells which we could clearly see bursting somewhere in the vicinity of the Monterey House and which we learned were from Kilpatrick's artillery, endeavoring to cut off our trains and prevent our retreat, gave the prisoners double assurance of release. Their hope of rescue being deferred at Monterey Springs, I instructed my Inspector-General to parole the officers and give them safeguard to return, binding them to render themselves prisoners of war at Richmond if they were not duly recognized by their government. Unfortunately, I was not permitted to release them at this point, and they were required to march with the rest of the prisoners.

A Colonel of a Maine regiment, Colonel Tilden, a splendid, gallant fellow, so appreciative, too, of the very few small courtesies which it has been possible to show him, asked that I cancel their paroles, the main object of which had been to avoid the terrors of the march, which I, in honor, did, of course.

. . . .

Late in the evening, after another trying day's march, we passed Waynesboro and, with a rest of only an hour or so, marched all night. At nine o'clock the following morning we reached Hagerstown but hurried on through to Williamsport. All along the road from Hagerstown to Williamsport were gruesome evidences of Kilpatrick's dash into Hagerstown — here a dead cavalryman, there a broken caisson, now and again a dead horse. I ought not to let your

75

beautiful eyes see through mine all these horrors, but some day, my darling, some day we'll strew roses and violets and lilies over them all, even over the memories of them. We'll listen to the resurrection that hope and faith and love voice in all the songs of nature. It will not be long, darling, for to-day the official news of the surrender of Vicksburg reached us. The tidings brought cheers from the prisoners and increased the sullen gloom of their guard.

I am directed to turn the prisoners over to General Imboden's command, who is to escort them to Staunton. Their final destination will, I suppose, be the old nine-room brick warehouse on Carey Street in Richmond, 'Libby & Sons — Ship Chandlers and Grocers' — a sign which I remember as a boy and associate with 'Cat' and 'Truant' and other boyish games. Always I shall like to remember it as a place to play, and not think of it as a living tomb. There will not, I fear, be many of my fellow-sufferers of the last few days who enter these awesome walls who will ever come forth alive.

The Potomac was so swollen by the rains which began on the fourth and still continue, that it was impossible to cross it at any of the neighboring fords. A rope ferry, the only means of crossing, made it slow and tedious, and every minute's delay, my darling, seems centuries, when I am on my way to you — to you.

I've had the great gratification of receiving a most complimentary and explanatory note from General Lee, which was highly appreciated by my men, and was an amelioration of their late imposed indignity of acting as provost-guard.

Jackerie has waited so long for my postscript that he has gone to sleep, and I have now not time to write it, but you will know that the most important thing is in the P. S. and this is love, — the love of

Your adoring
Soldier

On the March, July 12, 1863

XXIV

In which General Pickett Urges an Immediate Marriage *

THE short but terrible campaign is over, and we are again on this side of the Blue Ridge. Would that we had never crossed the Potomac, or that the splendid army which we had on our arrival in Pennsylvania had not been fought in detail. If the charge made by my gallant Virginians on the fatal third of July had been supported, or even if my other two brigades, Jenkins and Corse, had been with me, we would now, I believe, have been in Washington, and the war practically over. God in his wisdom has willed otherwise, and I fear there will be many more blooddrenched fields and broken hearts before the end does come.

I wrote to you on Wednesday by Colonel Harrison, who went to Richmond via Luray. I came on with my division, occupying both gaps of Front Royal,

*All except a fragment (see facsimile opposite this page) of the original of this letter has been lost. The above is quoted from *Pickett and his Men*, by La Salle Corbell Pickett. It is evident from comparison with the original fragment, and from the altered style, that the quoted letter has been to some extent changed. — A. C. I.

78

You will perceive my own darling Sallie that we are again this side of the Blue Ridge. The Campaign in Maryland and Penn was short but terrible. Would that we had never crossed the Potomac, or that the splendid army which we had on our arrival in Pennsylvania had not been fought in detail. If the charge made by my gallant Virginians on the fatal third of July had been supported, or even if my other two Brigades had been with me, we would now have been in Washington, and the war ended. But alas dearest God has willed otherwise. and the soul of our noble old

FRAGMENT OF LETTER OF JULY 23, 1863

Manassas and Chester, where we had a brilliant skir'
mish with the enemy. For three days and nights I
have been almost constantly in the saddle. Last night,
the 22d, I had a tent pitched, and sat down to a meal
at a camp'table, the first time since leaving Bunker
Hill. We had been going 'al fresco'. When we did
sleep it was with the heavens for a canopy and a
fence'rail for a pillow. We shall be here three or four
days, perhaps longer.

I thank the great and good God that he has spared
me to come back and claim your promise, and I pray
your womanly assistance in helping me to its *immedi'*
ate fulfilment. This is no time for ceremonies. The
future is all uncertain, and it is impossible for me to
call a moment my own. Again, with all the graves I
have left behind me, and with all the wretchedness
and misery this fated campaign has made, we would
not wish anything but a very silent, very quiet wed'
ding, planning only the sacrament and blessing of the
church, and, after that, back to my division and to
the blessing of those few of them who, by God's mira'
cle, were left.

I gave Colonel Harrison a gold luck'piece which
was a parting gift to me from the officers of the Pa'
cific, and told him to have it made into a wedding'

ring at Tyler's. I asked him to have engraved within "G. E. P. and S. C. Married ——," and to leave sufficient space for date and motto, which you would direct.

Your

Soldier

Culpeper C. H., July 23, 1863

XXV

In which General Pickett Pleads an Order

OLD Peter is to go to Tennessee to reënforce Bragg. He has placed his plans before the Sec-retary of War.

Now, my darling, I have just had a long pow-wow with him (Old Peter) who, 'old war-horse' as he is, has been in love himself, is still in love, will always be in love, and knows of our love — of our plighted troth — and knowing it, tells me it is his purpose to take me with him on this proposed expedition.

Now, my Sallie, your soldier is a soldier, and never, even to himself, questions an order. 'His not to reason why.' Darling, do you know what this means? Why, my little one, it means that you haven't one moment's respite. It means that you are to be Mrs. General George E. Pickett, my precious wife, right away. It means that you are to fufill your promise to 'come to me at a moment's notice'. Yours, too, *now*, 'not to reason why', but to obey and come at once. We can' not brook any delay, my sweetheart; so pack up your knapsack — never mind the rations and the ammu' nition — come! My Aunt Olivia and Uncle Andrew, Johnston and one of my staff and one of my couriers will meet you and your dear parents on this side of the Black Water and will escort you to Petersburg, where I shall be waiting at the train to meet you. I shall see you all to the hotel, where you will wait while your father, Bright and I get the license and make other necessary arrangements for our immediate mar' riage, which I have planned to take place at St. Paul's Church. Our old friend, Doctor Platt, will pronounce the words that make us one in the sight of the world. From the church, we will go to the depot, where a special train, having been arranged for us by our friend, Mr. Reuben Raglan, God bless him, will take us over to Richmond, where my little sister is wait' ing longingly to love and welcome my wife — her new sister.

My darling will realize how impossible it is for her soldier to consult with her and will forgive his bun' gling and awkwardness. Never mind, after this *she* shall do *all* the planning. Oh, what a heaven on earth is before us — if only this cruel war were over! A

General Pickett Pleads an Order

Dios. Forgive this business letter. Courier awaits.
You will come; I have no fear.

Forever, your

Soldier

I have intrusted my courier with some messages
and other instructions — the word key.

Headquarters, September 13, 1863

XXVI

Concerning General Pickett's Attempt to Capture Newbern

IT seems an age, my darling, since we rode away, leaving you and Mrs. Ransom* standing in that wonderful grove of maiden trees. I veil the annoying, disappointing scenes since then and see again the beautiful picture of my own bride,† clothed in white, in the greenery. "Mine — mine — all my own!" I said, invoking our Father's care of you. Oh, my love, all my happiness is in your hands, and as you love me, guard your precious self from all harm. I have you on my heart all the day.

Ransom sent on our letters from Kingston, via the Ugr.‡ I hope they reached you safely. Old Floyd § sent a most mysterious looking package to you and Mrs. Ransom, which he said you must both thank St. Paul for. In Floyd's opinion, St. Paul has as much to answer for as the great Apostle for whom he is named. Certainly in appearance he is as insignificant

---

* Wife of General Ransom.

† General Pickett was married to La Salle Corbell at Petersburg, September 15, 1863.

‡ Underground railway.   § Headquarters sutler.

looking as a horse as St. Paul has been described as a man, and while he has not had one, much less five, shipwrecks, he has had all manner of hairbreadth es, capes, hardships, indignities and a million times more stripes, all of which he has borne with Christian re, signation and endurance.

Well, dearest, my name is George and my patience and temper accord with the name. Our well-formed plans for the capture of Newbern miscarried. Hoke's, Clingman's, and Corse's Brigades, and Reid's Artil, lery, under my command were to make a feint — to threaten on the south side of the Neuse River. Dear, ing's Cavalry and three regiments of infantry under Dearing were to make a demonstration on the north side of the Neuse. Ransom, Barton, and Terry under Barton were to make the *real* attack, while we created a diversion and drew off the enemy. Simultaneously with our movements Colonel R. Taylor Wood was to take a naval force in small boats, make a night excur, sion down the Neuse and attack the gunboats. The soldiers were all jubilant, buoyant and hopeful. Every, thing was propitious; victory seemed sure. General Dearing's feint was successful — Hoke and Corse and Clingman crossed over, taking all the defenses and outworks in front — Wood's attack was a complete surprise, capturing a gunboat right under the guns of the fort — but, alas, the *real* attack by Barton *was not made!* We waited in deathlike suspense. Hour after hour of restless anxiety and impatience went by and yet no sound of a gun — and no message came to tell me why. The torture and suspense were unbearable. Newbern was ours — ours if — Well — hope died out and the dejection and despair of the men with their expectations dashed cannot be told. Barton's report to me to'day, through Bright, was that the 'defenses of the enemy were too formidable'. My orders to him were that if he found it impracticable to perform his part he was to come at once to me and let me try a *coup de main.*

As ever

Your

Soldier

XXVII

From the Lines, near Petersburg

Y OUR soldier breathes easier this morning, my
darling. A great load is lifted. Haygood's brave
South Carolina Brigade came in yesterday, thank God,
and I stationed them at Port Walthall Junction. This
will keep the connection between Petersburg and
Richmond open. Wise's Brigade got in to-day and
was sent out toward City Point.

For nights I have not closed my eyes. How could
I, with a whole city full of helpless, defenseless women
and children at the mercy of an oncoming army?
Butler's whole force, in transports protected by his
gunboats, landed at City Point and Bermuda Hundred, and no army here to meet them! Not enough
soldiers, boys and old men all put together, even for
picket duty!

Come to think of it, my prettice, you must have
been up all night to have gotten up and sent out such
a basket of goodies, and baked and buttered such a lot
of biscuit, and made so many jugs of coffee as came
this morning. My, I tell you it all tasted good, and the
coffee — well, no Mocha or Java ever tasted half so

good as this rye-sweet-potato blend! And think of your thoughtfulness in wrapping blankets around the jugs to keep the coffee hot. Bless your thoughtful heart! You are, without doubt, the dearest, most indefatigable little piece of perfection that ever rode a horse or buttered a biscuit or plucked a flower or ever did anything else, as to that. Then those hyacinths and geranium leaves. Who else in all this nerve-racking, starving, perilous time would have thought of gathering flowers? My boy Bob, the loyal but unappreciative scamp, apologetically took out the baskets, which were apparently filled with the yet dew-kissed fragrant flowers, and said:

" Miss Sallie, Marse George, done en sont you all dese yer endoubled hyacinfs. En I axed her huccome she sont 'em; but she aint say. So ef you all don't lak 'em you-all mus' 'scuse her fum it en put all de blame 'pon me. En anyhow, Marse George, ef you cyan't eat dese hyacinfses ner w'ar 'em ner shoot de Yankees wid 'em, dey suttinly does smell good and dey sho' is pretty."

Mrs. Stratton and Mrs. Johnson sent out large hampers, too, to us. They came just after we had gotten through with your baskets, so we passed them on to the others.

Near Petersburg

And now, my darling, what on earth did you mean by saying, " Never mind," as you said good-by and rode away yesterday. It troubled me all night. I wanted to follow after you and ask you what you meant, but couldn't. I would have jumped on Lucy and ridden into Petersburg and found out if it had been *possible* for me to leave. I was so troubled about it that I was almost tempted to come in anyhow. But for the life of me, little one, I couldn't think of any reason why you should say, "Never mind," to *me*. Were you aggrieved, my darling, because your blundering old soldier told you there was no necessity for your coming out to bring the dispatches, any longer; that, thank heaven, the recruits and reënforcements were coming in now, and that we could manage all right? I did not mean to hurt you, dear. I hoped you'd send a line by Bob telling me what you meant and why you had said it, but when I asked him if you had written, he said:

" Yas, Suh, Marse George, 'course de mistis is done en writ a letter er answer er sumpin'; but ef she done did it, den I mus' er forgot ter fotch it, bein' ez I wuz in sich a hurry ter git yere in time dis mornin', a-startin' befo' daybre'k. En den dis ebenin' a-gittin' de basket en papers en milk en things

89

ready in sich a hurry agin, I mus' er forgot de letter agin."

Now, please, my darling, send Bob back *right away* with a nice letter and tell your soldier that you did not mean anything by saying, "Never mind," to him, for he loves you with all his heart and would not wound or disappoint or offend you for anything in the world.

Your

Soldier

On the Lines, May 7, 1864

XXVIII

In the Battle-Line, before Cold Harbor

BAIRD has just come in from the lines, my dar⸗
ling wife, and reports that all is well. I came in
about eleven and was lying in my tent all alone, think⸗
ing of you, and while I builded wonderful castles I was
serenading you with the songs I love.

I think I had finished all the songs I had ever sung
to you, and when Baird came in my thoughts had
wandered to the Salmon⸗Illahie and I was singing
Anne Boleyn's song, 'Oh Death, Rock Me Asleep',
which was taught me by my friend, Captain G. P.
Hornby, of Her Majesty's ship *Tribune*, away out in
San Juan Island on the Pacific Coast in 1859. I do not
know why I was singing this song, except that it is
beautiful and one of the finest and sweetest of melo⸗
dies. Both the air and words were written by poor,
unfortunate Anne Boleyn. I know but one verse — if
Hornby ever knew other verses he had forgotten
them — but the one I know is appealing. I will write
it for you, if I may:

> "Oh, Death, rock me asleep! Bring me to quiet and rest;
> Let pass my weary, guiltless life out of my careful breast;

Toll on the passing bell, ring out my doleful knell;
Let thy sound my death tell. Death doth draw me,
Death doth draw me. There is no remedy."

Baird stopped outside and listened and then came in, asking permission to order Bob to light the dips, and saying, "Please, Sir, Marse George, when you sing that song I haven't got a friend in the world. I'm lonesome and feel creeps and see spooks and, what's worse, I don't know whether I am Anne Boleyn her-self, or am myself responsible for all poor Anne's sorrows and death."

So I stopped singing and am writing to tell you a great secret, which is — I love you. Some day when we are happy — so happy that nothing could make us any happier — I'll sing this song to you.

Last night there was a night attack. Several of the men were wounded slightly; but the face of one — perhaps seriously wounded — haunts me. He is a boy with golden brown curls — somebody's darling. To-night, we made a capture of the Federal pickets, sweeping their rifle-pits for more than a hundred yards and taking a hundred and thirty-six prisoners. You know our lines are so close together in many places that we, the Yankees and my men, can with voices raised carry on a conversation.

War and its horrors, and yet I sing and whistle.

In the Battle-Line

Oh, my sweetheart, if only this wicked war were over so that we could in peace and quiet tranquilly finish the book of Love which we have but just begun.

Adios now. I see old Jackerie in the flap with his pack and bag, his wonted grace and patience, his *dolce-far-niente* eyes and soft, southern Italian voice, saying, "No hulla-nonenty." But I must hurry, for he starts at daybreak and it is now past midnight.

Lovingly now and forever,

Your

Soldier

In Camp, May — 1864

XXIX

Before Cold Harbor

I HAVE just this moment returned from a visit to the lines, where I have been since early this morning. To-day, my precious, has only been a duplicate of yesterday. Thank God I have at last, if not too late, gotten a line laid out on my right flank. The 'Ides of March' are upon us! Grant says he intends taking his 4th of July dinner in Richmond. I have been hard at work, my pet, trying in every way with my limited force to strengthen my front. This has been done by my division, but on the right of my line, towards the Appomattox, it has been impossible for me to accomplish anything, troops have been put in and removed, so often. However, now I know what I have to overcome, and will try and do it — I hate uncertainties.

Your sweet letter of this morning came as a true messenger of love. I was so very, very anxious about you. My own wife, keep up your heart bravely, and think of your husband who lives but for you. I would, my prettice, give any thing in the world — any thing — to see you this evening. God knows, I do

Before Cold Harbor

want to kiss you and call you my own. Remember how much I am longing for you. A Dios, my Sallie.

I send you by this mail a little butter. It is all I can find. I had a pretty little flower, but it withered in the intensely hot sun.

Your devoted

Soldier

May (or June), 1864

XXX

Concerning the Battle of Cold Harbor

HERE we are still, my Sallie. My division is stationed with the rest of the First Corps be-tween new and old Cold Harbor. Old Peter, having been wounded in the Wilderness, Anderson has been put in command of the First Corps. Grant has been appointed Lieutenant General and has arrived at nearly the same point in his march down the river that McClellan reached in his upward progress in '62. Over a crimson road both armies have returned to Cold Harbor. The Wilderness, alas, is one vast grave-yard where sleep thousands of Grant's soldiers; but Grant, like our Stonewall, is 'fighting not to save lives, but country'.

For the second time now Cold Harbor has become a battle-ground. Two years ago it furnished the field for the battle of Gaines's Mill (which the Yankees called Cold Harbor) where your soldier was wounded. Does it seem to you as long ago as two years, my dar-ling? To me, it seems but yesterday that I lay in Rich-mond at my little sister's and you came to see me, blessing and cheering me. I can feel now the soft touch of your little white hands, as you gently stroked and soothed my wounded shoulder and swollen arm and hand. Do you remember one afternoon while you were reading from Moore's melodies (not that I heard or took in the meaning of a single word of them, for I only heard the music of your wonderful voice and saw the long, dark lashes caressing the words which those cherry red lips were uttering) that our dear old Stonewall was announced? Of course I knew his calling was out of the usual, and I was honored and gratified by his coming; but any guest was unwelcome if I had to share with him my precious. I remember that you marked the place you were reading with your dainty, citise scented handkerchief, which I stole, and still have. You and my sister were about to withdraw; but both the General and I urged you to remain. I shall always hold sacred 'Old Jack's' visit and remember its every detail.

Do you recall how indignant our maidservant was at what she supposed a reflection upon the mint juleps she was serving, when the uncompromising, stern old Puritan declined, saying, "Take that liquor away; I never touch strong drink. I like it too well to fool with it, and no man's strength is strong enough to touch that stuff with impunity."? Do you remember how poor Julie curtsied, but humbly, vigorously defending her juleps, replying, " 'Scuse me, Marse Gen'ul Jackson, but dese yer drams ain't got no empunities in 'em, Suh. Nor, Suh. Braxton done en mek 'em out'n weall's ve'y bes' old London Dock brandy."?

Old Jackerie brought me your letter on the first, just after the Yankees' attack on Hoke and Kershaw, breaking their outer lines. That night Grant transferred his right to a point beyond Cold Harbor. On the afternoon of the second Marse Robert ordered an assault on Grant's right; but old Jubal* found it invincible and went to work erecting defenses. I believe it was old Jube who gave Marse Robert the title of 'OldSpadesLee', or 'Old Ace of Spades', because of his incessant activity in throwing up defenses, trenches, breastworks, etc. This morning Grant made an assault along the entire six miles of our line, and our guns opened a counter attack, followed by advance skirmishes of my division. The whole Confederate line poured a stream of fire, and thousands of Grant's soldiers have gone to reënforce the army of the dead.

* General Early.

The Battle of Cold Harbor

Oh, this is all a weary, long mistake. May the merciful and true God wield power to end it ere another day passes!

Your

Soldier

I love you — love you — love you.

Cold Harbor, June 3, 1864

XXXI

After General Lee had Congratulated 'Pickett's Men' for Gallantry

OUTSIDE, my prettice, the band has been play-ing 'The Harp That Once through Tara's Halls', 'Blue Juniata', 'Sweet and Low', 'Lorelei', 'Last Night the Nightingale Woke Me', 'Nellie Gray', 'Massa's in the Cold, Cold Ground'; and inside I have been softly singing them all to you, to your spirit far away. Now they have wound up with 'Alice, Where Art Thou?' which might have set me wondering if it had not been the hour we each seek to be alone that we may bring our souls in touch. So I knew that thou wert with me.

This morning Tom Friend brought me a weesome package of tea, which he wishes sent to you. "One of the men," he said, "swapped his tobacco for it." If the whole universe were mine, I'd lay it at your feet, for love has builded in my heart three altars for thy worship — one to Faith, one to Hope, one to Service — and you, my Goddess whom I worship, must feed my faith, illumine my hope and command my service.

General Lee's Congratulations

This morning, for reasons which you will presently note, I was thinking of our ever memorable ride from Petersburg. Its anxieties and pleasures, your indomitable pluck and merry laughter on that day pass before me, making me shudder with fear or thrill with happiness. It was on your birthday, you remember, and Beauregard had been forced to leave his intrenchments at early daylight, and Butler had walked into them and had succeeded in reaching the Richmond and Petersburg Railroad and was destroying the track when the advance guard of my division ran him off. I had left you in the rear and had gone on about a quarter of a mile in advance of my division and was riding quietly along with the members of my staff and General R. H. Anderson, who was then commanding the corps. We were some ten miles or so from Petersburg when we were ambushed and fired into by a portion of Butler's troops. Hunton's Brigade was followed up by my other brigades, and we drove the enemy back toward Bermuda Hundred, where they at once tried to hold the line given up by Beauregard, but were stopped by my men who retook the whole line.

This gallant and unexpected action so pleased Marse Robert that he yesterday had published the inclosed notice, a copy of which I send you that you may be reminded of my glorious, fearless men who yet survived that awful third of July where so many of their comrades were left to sleep. The line of breastworks which they took and to which Marse Robert refers in the notice inclosed is most important, as the main line of defense between Richmond and Petersburg and opposing any advance of the enemy upon the peninsula of Bermuda Hundred.

Now my darling sees why I am thinking of that 16th of May. It was because she, though Marse Robert doesn't know it, comes in for a share of his praise. I am thinking of you every minute and wish that I could ride in, if only for an hour between sundown and midnight, to see you; but, to use Mr. Lincoln's expressive words, Grant is so 'infernally interruptious' that I am afraid to take the risk.

And now, my strayed angel of the skies, my own, good night. May all blessings bless you, all sunshine shine for you, all angels guard you, all that is good take care of you and all heaven help me to be worthy of you.

Forever and ever

Your

Soldier

Headquarters, June 18, 1864

GENERAL LEE'S CONGRATULATIONS

Clay's House, 5:30 P. M., June 17, 1864

LIEUTENANT-GENERAL R. H. ANDERSON,
  Commanding Longstreet's Corps.

GENERAL:

I take great pleasure in presenting to you my congratulations upon the conduct of the men of your corps. I believe they will carry anything they are put against. We tried very hard to stop Pickett's men from capturing the breastworks of the enemy, but could not do it. I hope his loss has been small.

I am, with respect, your obedient servant,

R. E. LEE, General.

XXXII

When Butler Burned General Pickett's Old Home

WAS my letter of yesterday strenuous? Well, it was a strenuous day, full of rumors and contradictions. And yet in spite of it I managed to sandwich in between the shelling and the movement of the fleet and the distinguished visitors the ever new and true story of my love; but I had only time to make the bare announcement at the close of that letter that Butler had burned our home * the day before. If it had been burned in line of battle, it would have been all right; but it was not. It was burned by Butler at a great expense to the Government and in revenge for having been outgeneraled by a little handful of my men at Petersburg and for Grant's telegram to Mr. Lincoln, saying, "Pickett has bottled up Butler at Petersburg."

Mr. Sims, who has been our overseer ever since I can remember, came up from Turkey Island this morning to tell me all about it. The poor old fellow loved the old place and is heartbroken over its destruc-

* Turkey Island, in Henrico County.

tion. He says they first looted the house and then
shelled and burned it, together with the barn and
stables. He is very bitter and vindictive and vows all
manner of eternal vengeance. The poor old chap is
sensitive because I did not rave and rage with him,
and resents what he considers my indifference. He
gave me the benefit of all the swear words in his vocabulary when I tried to make him understand that
there are weightier things and subjects of greater moment than the mere loss of personal property.

"'Personal property!'" he quoted indignantly.
"Why, Turkey Island was your ma's and pa's and
their ma's and pa's before 'em. Think of them big oaks,
them maiden trees, the river and everything! Think
of all the big men that's set 'round that old mahogany
table and jingled their glasses at that big old sideboard!
'Personal property!' Why, when you was just a turn
ing six your pa and me showed you the very halting
place whar in January, 1781, that traitor, Benedict
Arnold, stopped on his march to Richmond after he
had come up with the fleet at Jamestown and then
went on to Westover. 'Personal property!' Why, I remember the very day we sot you up in the crotch of that
great old oak tree under which Governor Jefferson and
Mr. Edmund Randolph 'lighted from their fillies and

tied them to one of the limbs till they could walk a piece and see for themselves that old monument put up in 1711, eleven years before that time, to show how much devilment a river could do if it had the elements to help it. 'Personal property!' Why, Sir, there wan't a picture or a piece of furniture or a statuary in that old home that wan't only seasoned with age, but had a store of valuableness to it besides, and you passive and peaceable, taking the news all quiet as if it had been nothing but a fence rail burnt up, and telling me to my face, and me a-bustin' out with damnation from every pore, that you had heard of the fire, that Mr. Enroughty had reported the burning of Turkey Island yesterday! 'Reported!' 'Personal property!' I wonder if a man's soul is personal property. Well, if it is and Mr. Satan should ever report to me that he wanted any help to keep up his fire to burn Mr. Butler's, or any of his kind of personal property, he would know where to get it!"

Poor Mr. Sims! I've sent him with one of my couriers to find some of his friends in the trenches, where I hope he will work off some of his wrath over Butler and his kind and my unfortunate phrase 'personal property'. Of course you know, my darling, that I am not unmindful of the sacredness of the old home and that I grieve that it has been destroyed, but we will build us another home, won't we? The river is there, and some of the old trees are left. And if God should bless us with a son I shall, when he is as old as I was then, take him under this same old historic tree that Mr. Sims speaks of and tell him in the very language of my father some of the old stories he used to tell me, and introduce him to the great men of those days as my father made me acquainted with them. I can hear him now say:

"My son, there was Madison, a very, very small man with introverted eyes and ample forehead. He dressed always in a surtout of brown, which was generally dusty and oftener than otherwise faded and shabby. Judge Marshall was very tall and commanding and revolutionary and patriarchal in appearance. He had fine expressive eyes and dressed always in a well-fitting surtout of blue. Mr. John Randolph was puny and frail and most uncommon looking. He was swarthy and wrinkled, with eyes as brilliant as stars of the first magnitude. Watkins Leigh was unusually distinguished in appearance. Tazewell was tall and fine looking; but Mr. Monroe was very wrinkled and weather-beaten and so exceedingly awkward that he stumbled over his own feet and walked on everyone else's. Governor Giles used a crutch always and talked like molasses in July."

My father never used made-up words or a children's vocabulary in describing to me men and events. He would say, "Words are things, my son. I want you to know them and not be like the British officer who, when he and some of his command were taken prisoners and were told by their captors that they were to be paroled, demanded in great terror and consternation, 'Pray, what kind of death is that?'"

Oh, my Sallie, I dream of the happy days when you will be the fair mistress of Turkey Island, under those old trees, with the James River always before us and love always with us. As the sun in the firmament, so is love in the world — love, the life of the spirit, the root of every virtuous action. It enhanceth prosperity, easeth adversity and maketh of the slightest twist a Gordian knot. It gives vigor to the atmosphere, fragrance to the flower, color to the rainbow, zest to life, music to laughter, and oh, such laughter as yours, my own, my beautiful. I love you with all my heart and soul and mind and being. A Dios. Keep this love close.

Your
Soldier

Headquarters, June —, 1864

XXXIII

Upon Hearing of the Birth of the 'Little General'

GOD bless you, little Mother of our boy — bless and keep you. Heaven in all its glory shine upon you; Eden's flowers bloom eternal for you. Al' most with every breath since the message came, re' lieving my anxiety and telling me that my darling lived and that a little baby had been born to us, I have been a baby myself. Though I have known all these months that from across Love's enchanted land this little child was on its way to our twin souls, now that God's promise is fulfilled and it has come, I can't be' lieve it. As I think of it I feel the stir of Paradise in my senses, and my spirit goes up in thankfulness to God for this, His highest and best — the one perfect flower in the garden of life — Love.

Blinding tears rolled down my cheeks, my sweet' heart, as I read the glad tidings. And a feeling so new, so strange, came over me that I asked of the angels what it could be and whence came the strains of ce lestial music which filled my soul, and what were the great, grand, stirring hosannas and the soft, tender, sweet adagios that circled round and round, warmed my every vein, beat in my every pulse. And — oh, little Mother of my boy — the echoing answer came — "A little baby has been born to you, and he and the new born Mother live."

I wanted to fly to you both, kneel by your bedside, take your hand and his little hand, our baby's, in mine and lift up hearts in thankfulness to the Heavenly Throne. But when I applied to the great Tyee for a pass to Richmond, saying, "My son was born this morning," he replied, "Your country was born almost a hundred years ago." It was the first word suggestive of reproach that Marse Robert ever spoke to me; but he was right, and I was reckless to ask.

Things may be quieter to morrow, sweetheart, perhaps even to night, and I may be able to come in for an hour. I must not write another word, though I want to write on and on and send messages and kisses to our boy and to caution the little Mother to be careful and to tell her she is ten thousand times more precious than ever — but I must not.

Forever lovingly

Your

Soldier

July 17, 1864 — Our boy's birthday
Blessed Day

XXXIV

On the Occasion of General Pickett's First Visit to his Son

MY men had all heard of the arrival of the 'Little General', as they call him, and when I was riding out of camp last night to surrender to him, I noticed the bonfires which were being kindled all along my lines and knew that my loyal, loving men were lighting them in honor of my son. But I did not know till this morning that dear old Ingalls, at Grant's suggestion, had kindled a light on their side of the lines, too, and I was overcome with emotion when I learned of it. To-day their note of congratulation, marked unofficial, which I inclose, came to me through the lines. You must keep it for the baby, with the pass and note of Marse Robert which I put into its little clenched hand.

"Baby!" Can it be true, my darling? Heaven knows no deeper devotion, no deeper gratitude, than that which filled my heart when I realized that the golden dream of life had come to pass — was true.

I see still the moss rose bud left by the *Blumen-Engel* as a *bescheidenen Schmuck* of his love nestling in your snow-white arms and the long, dark lashes kissing your cheeks as you look down upon it. I still feel the mystic power of the grasp of its tiny rose leaf fingers clutched around my own.

But I must not write another word — not one.

Lovingly,

Your

Soldier

In Camp, July 19, 1864

To GEORGE PICKETT:
We are sending congratulations to you, to the young mother and the young recruit.

GRANT, INGALLS, SUCKLEY

July 18, 1864

XXXV

Concerning Confederate Food and Confederate Prices

SISTER'S letter came this morning with the glad tidings that my precious wife was better. Please thank her for it. Two of my brigadiers are here and I can't keep our Italian waiting, so will not be able to write at length. I enclose a letter to you from your Mother. I am delighted to hear that your Father is well. How pleased they will be when they get the next news — won't they, my own?

I send in ice, berries, and some apples — the latter are not ripe by any means, but may do for cooking. Captain Bright sends some squabs. He will send my Sallie two more within a week.

Your husband will look round for what he can, but this country is overrun. I sent out a little silver this morning to get some butter, and was charged one dollar and a half a pound, at the rate of thirty dollars a pound in Confederate. Twelve dollars a piece for chickens, in notes. People are certainly crazy! I will write Milligan and ask him what the chances are of

getting a wagon load of things up from Chuckatuck
— but I am almost afraid to trust one through.

Oh, my Sallie, I do want to see you so much. I have
been right sick for a day or two past, but am better to-
day. I had no business to be sick and low spirited,
when God has been so good to us. I fancy, could I only
have seen my own faithful loving wife, and told her
what was uppermost in my mind that I would have
gotten well. Dearest, I will try and get in some time
this week. A Dios, my sweet. Kiss the little George
for me.

Ever, darling of my heart,

Your own

Soldier

In Camp, August —, 1864

XXXVI

Upon Returning from a Ride with General Lee

I HAVE but a few moments since, my pretty one, returned from a ride with the Tyee up one hill and down the other. The enemy occupied Dutch Gap last evening. This is higher up the river than I am and I had expected the Navy to take care of our rear but they have allowed them to come in, and now I have to stretch out my India rubber division.

Well, I *have* to do it. The General did not seem in a remarkably good humor — with the news from Mobile and Bradley, Johnson in the valley, and this impudence of the Yankees in crawling up behind us.

I am so glad, my own, that you are better — thank the good God for it.

I send you a chicken, a cup of salt, likewise an apple — one single one. Your friend, Miss Gamble, radiant with a white frock and smiles, sent it to me (*didn't give it*) with her compliments last night.

Good-bye, sweet one.

Ever your own

Soldier

Headquarters, August —, 1864

XXXVII

Concerning the Gossip of General Pickett's Servant, George

I LEFT my Garden of Eden, my darling, 'with many a pause and longing glance behind'; but out in the midst of this terrible conflict to which I have come, your love is with me, shielding and blessing me.

I reached camp just before daybreak. George hustled around and made me a pot of 'sho'nough coffee wid no bedultrement in it'. And while I drank my coffee he kept off the flies — which, early as it was, had begun to be very sociable — entertaining me the while with news of the camp and his own views on current events.

"You know, Marse George," he began, "po' Rob ert, Marse Jefferson Davis' mos' betrusted servant, is done en bruck out thick all ober wid de smallpox, en dar ain' no tellin' how many er de President's frien's en 'quaintances po' Robert is done en kernockulated wid it, kaze po' Robert wuz moughty sociable en familious wid all de President's frien's. I suttinly hopes dat you en Gen'l Lee en Gen'l Heth is gwine ter 'scape. I wuz so upsot, Marse George, by dis news

116

'bout po' Robert dat I couldn' sleep, en I got out be-
hime de tent en listened ter de officers a talkin' wid
dar moufs en gesticulatin' 'bout de way t'ings wuz
gwine.

"Some er 'em said how ef Marse Albert Sydney
Johnston hadn't been kilt at Shiloh, en ef Marse Joe
Johnston hadn't been wounded at Seben Pines, en
ef you had been s'po'ted at Gettysburg, dat t'ings
wouldn't be lak dey wuz now. Den one er de officers
say, ' Yes — yes, en ef all er dem folks down dar in
New 'Leans dat commit suicide wid darse'fs, 'count
er ole Butler's pusecution en hangin's en yuther devil
ments, had er kilt him fust fo' dey kilt deyse'fs dey'd
er had sumpin ter die fer, en de ole rascal wouldn' be
down yere now adiggin' dis Dutch-Gap-Canal en
givin ev'body ague en fever turnin' up de earf!' Den
one er de preacher officers say, ' Well, my frien's, de
trouble is, we all don' pray nuf!' Den Marse Charley
spuck up en say, ' Didn' Gen'l Jackson pray nuf fer
us all, Colonel?' Nur one say, ' Yes, Charley, but he
didn' dust his knees off when he wuz through. He
fergit dat bein' clean wuz nex' ter being Godlisome.'
Den a nur one say, ' Well, but dar's ole Gen'l Pember
ton en Gen'l Kershaw. Dey wuz particular wid dar
clothes en dey prayed all right.' Den Gen'l Corse he

spuck up en say, 'Yes, but dey bofe t'ink *too much* 'bout dar 'pearance. Dey'd begin to dus' en dus' dar knees fo' dey said, "Amen." En dat showed dar hearts wan't in dar prayers.'

"En gwine back, Marse George, ter dat Dutch Gap Canal, you know Colonel Mayo's nigger, Big Joe, en sebenteen mo' er de camp niggers is done en gone cross de river ter jine de Yankee Army en he'p de res' er dem Yankee nigger soldiers ter dig dat canal ditch dey's diggin' er 'count er all dat extra money en extra drams en coffee en yuther extras Gen'l Butler promise ter give 'em. Now, Marse George, you done know dat dat's projickin' wid de Lord's handy wuks, en sumpin mousterious en turrble's gwine ter happen ter dem niggers, fer diggin' dat canal sho'ly is gwine ag'inst de judgment er de Lord, fer ef de Lord had er wanted de Jeemes River ter a j'ined on ter itse'f He'd a j'ined it. He 'ou'dn't a put a little slice er land in be twixt. En sho's you bawn projickin' wid de Lord's wuk en unj'inin' whut He's j'ined ain't a gwine ter bring dem niggers no proskerity."

Having finished my breakfast George went out to get breakfast for the mess, and before they had assembled I had cleared off my desk and written several letters. All made affectionate inquiries for you and our little son, though some of them did not know that I had ridden in last night until I told them.

I must go now, my Sallie, and ride around the lines and make my report, but will add a few more words later on. So a Dios till then.

. . . .

Well, my darling, we have had a most exciting day. Marse Robert came out. He was restive and very, very silent. We had just paid our respects to Butler's diggers when he arrived. The device we used in so doing was a new one or rather a very old one newly revived. It was a mortar battery hidden in the bushes, invisible to the enemy, and easily shifted from one hiding place to the other. It used to be the only way in which shells could be thrown. It throws these shells high in the air, and they fall by their own weight without the least warning of their coming. There is no screaming or squealing sound like that made by our modern shells. They fall almost as silently as a snowflake falls, and it seems to me almost barbarous to drop these silent, ghostly missiles down upon those light-hearted, happy-go-lucky negroes, for I learn that it is they that are doing the digging. Butler, with promise of extra pay for extra work and extra danger, has induced four hundred of his colored soldiers to volunteer to sheathe their swords and take up the shovel and go to digging.

The bank to be cut through is only about five feet at the highest point. The canal is to be where the James makes a great bend just above Dutch Gap, in-closing a point of land perhaps half a mile wide and about three miles in length and which at the neck is only five hundred yards across from river to river. Their canal would thus save them six miles and would allow their gunboats to go up the James without run-ning the gauntlet of our Howlett guns, our sunken torpedoes et cetera. And as our left is all at the turn of the bend, they would not have to traverse the open river in search of an exposed water channel. It is strange that some of our brilliant engineers haven't made this near cut years ago. As for me, I should en-courage Butler and his River Improvement Company, and cease throwing these stealthy shells whose silent fall heralds a sudden roar of explosion that strikes ter-ror to my soul. The canal will be an advantage to us, and Butler, in digging it for us, may in part atone for the many homes he has destroyed, mine among them.

Well, my own, if you were not the best of all good women, as well as the most beautiful of all beautiful women and the most patient of all patient women, you

General Pickett's Servant

would weary of so tiresome a soldier, who takes away the fragrance of flowers and the glory of love and sends back the echo of war and its sorrows and the babble of a loyal old cook who wouldn't be sold and wouldn't run away and whom I was obliged to per mit to be credited to me in order to save him — the only negro I own — but, come to think of it, he owns me.

Forever and ever

Your

Soldier

In Camp, August —, 1864

XXXVIII

After an Evening Spent at the 'White House' of the Confederacy

YOU will be glad, my darling wife, that the 'powwow' with 'the Powers that be' was most satisfactory.

After the evening consultation I called on the ladies at the 'White House' and at the most earnest entreaty and solicitation of Mrs. Davis and her sister, Miss Howell, dined with them. Poor Mr. Davis looks tired and anxious, but he spoke so hopefully of our success that, knowing, as he must know, our status, the condition of our army, etc., I should have thought that he was aware of something hopeful of which we are ignorant if he had not said later, when foreign intervention was being discussed, that he 'believed that England and, in fact, all the foreign powers were like the woman who saw her husband fighting a bear — she didn't care a continental which was whipped, but she'd be the best pleased if both were'.

The dinner, my Sallie, was beautiful, and so abun- dant were its luxuries that I marveled greatly, know- ing, as I do, how difficult it is with most of us to get

LA SALLE CORBELL PICKETT
From a drawing by Mrs. L. M. Leisenring

even a little tea or coffee or salt. As usual, Mrs. Davis
was vivacious and entertaining. She amusingly described her rescue of a little orphan negro from a
'great black brute' who had constituted himself the
boy's guardian. She told how she had him washed
and combed and dressed in a suit of little Joe's clothes,
and how, while he was proud of the clothes, he was
a thousand times prouder of, and more grateful for,
the cuts and bruises which his self-appointed guardian
had given him and which, upon all occasions, he tri-
umphantly exhibited as medals of honor. She said
that the little rascal was greatly troubled when the
cuts were finally healed and tried to reopen them with
a dog knife which was taken away. He was then re-
proved and forbidden to make over his wounds.

"Oh, Lordy," he howled, "ef you-all teks my
sores 'way fum me I won't hab nuttin' 'tall ter show
ter all de comp'ny, en I won't hab a single ting ter
mek 'em all sorry 'bout, en nuttin' ter mek 'em gib
me no mo' tings. Oh, Lordy, I'd ruther you'd all
whop me dan notter let me hab my sores no mo'."

With her keen sense of humor Mrs. Davis told us
how, when learning that one after another of her
maids was being bribed by the Yankees with money
and promises to betray the family and come over to

the other side, she would, pretending ignorance of the intention, give them food for imagination, reciting for their repetition the most impossible, outlandish stories, some of which she told us. She said that Betty, the last one of her maids to go, was such an excellent maid and so hard to replace that as soon as she began to show her prosperity, appearing with silks and jewels and then with gold and notes, she had tried, without letting Betty suspect her intention, to offer her inducements to remain, but had failed. Betty, she said, was superior to her class, however, and showed her consideration by offering Miss Howell part of the as yet unearned bribe, and assuring her that 'ef eber she did git de chance ter tell dem dar Yankees 'bout dey'all she suttinly wan't gwine tell 'em none er de awful scand'lus tings she en Mis' Davis was all de time a'doin' en dat dey'all does. *No*, she was a'gwine ter mek de best er hit en leave outn de worse.'

Mrs. Davis said she was so depressed after Betty's departure and in such dire need of mental soothing syrup that she went into retirement with 'Adam Bede', 'A Country Gentleman in Town' and 'Elective Affinities'. Did you ever, my darling!

Mr. Judah P. Benjamin and Dr. Minnegerode were the only other guests. Mr. Benjamin's usually wonderful, judicial mind and depressing dignity were not in evidence. He did rather reproachfully express his astonishment that Mr. Davis should be bowed down with grief by the adverse criticisms of those he was trying to serve, and that he should care a bauble for their accusations of nepotism and the more absurd charge of leaving his cotton to be bought by the Yankees. He ended by saying that he continually had to remind Mr. Davis of that exceedingly good man, Christ. You know, my own, Benjamin was born at St. Croix in the West Indies, of Jewish parents.

What a gossip your husband is, my Sallie, but I promised to write my beautiful tyrant every day, everything I said or did or that anyone else said or did, and I have.

Forever and ever

Your

Soldier

Richmond, January 25, 1865

XXXIX

In the Dark Days before the End

THIS morning at breakfast, my darling Sallie, when you suggested having an oyster roast for my officers after our conference to night, I said that I feared we should not have enough oysters. Our old hunter, Gossett, has just brought in a fine large wild turkey, and with that and the three bushels of oysters which your uncle, Colonel Phillips, sent I think we can get up a fine supper. Don't you, my marvel of a housekeeper? I hope you can, and hope, too, that the good cheer it will provide will help us to new and encouraging suggestions, for, as hopeful as I always am, even *my* heart is in my boots.

On every side gloom, dissatisfaction and disap pointment seem to have settled over all, men and officers alike, because of the unsuccessful termination of the Peace Conference on board the *River Queen* on the fatal third. The anxious, despairing faces I see everywhere bespeak heavy hearts. Our commission ers knew that we were gasping our last gasp and that the Peace Conference was a forlorn hope. Because of the informality of the conference and my know

126

ledge of Mr. Lincoln, his humanity, his broad nature, his warm heart, I did believe he would take advantage of this very informality and spring some wise, superhuman surprise which would, somehow, restore peace and in time insure unity. Now, heaven help us, it will be war to the knife, with the knife no longer keen, the thrust of the arm no longer strong, the certainty that when peace comes it will follow the tread of the conqueror —

Your

Soldier

Howlett House on Bermuda Hundred Lines, January 28, 1865

XL

Written in Defeat, after the Battle of Five Forks

IT is long past the midnight hour and, like a boy, I have been reading over your dear, cheery letter, caressing the written page because it has been touched by your hand.

All is quiet now, but soon all will be bustle, for we march at daylight. Oh, my darling, were there ever such men as those of my division? This morning after the review I thanked them for their valiant services yesterday on the first of April, never to be forgotten by any of us, when, to my mind, they fought one of the most desperate battles of the whole war. Their answer to me was cheer after cheer, one after another calling out, "That's all right, Marse George!" and "We only followed you!" Then in the midst of these calls, silencing them, rose loud and clear dear old Gentry's voice, singing the old hymn which they all knew I loved:

> "Guide me, oh, thou great Jehovah,
> Pilgrim through this barren land."

Voice after voice joined in till from all along the line the plea rang forth:

Written in Defeat

"Be my sword and shield and banner,
Be the Lord my righteousness."

I do not think, my Sallie, the tears sounded in my voice as it mingled with theirs; but they were in my eyes, and there was something new in my heart.

When the last line had been sung, I gave the order to march, proceeding to this point where I had expected to cross the Appomattox and rejoin the main army. While we were at a halt here orders came from General R. H. Anderson to report to him at Sutherland's Tavern.

Just after mailing my letter to you at Five Forks, telling you of our long, continuous march of eighteen hours and of the strenuous hours following those, where I had, because of exigent circumstances, been induced to fall back at daylight, I received a dispatch from the great Tyee telling me to "hold Five Forks at all hazards to prevent the enemy from striking the south side railroad." This dispatch was in reply to one I had sent to him reporting the state of affairs and that the enemy were trying to get in between the army and my command, and asking that diversion be made at once or I should be isolated.

I had had all trains parked in the rear of Hatcher's Run and much preferred that position, but, from the

General's dispatch, supposed that he intended sending reënforcements. I immediately formed line of battle upon the White Oak Road and set my men to throwing up temporary breastworks. Pine trees were felled, a ditch dug and the earth thrown up behind the logs. The men, God bless them, though weary and hungry, sang as they felled and dug. Three times in the three hours their labors were suspended because of attack from the front; but they as cheerily returned to their digging and to their ' Annie Laurie' and ' Dixie' as if they were banking roses for a festival.

Five Forks is situated in a flat, thickly wooded country and is simply a crossing at right angles of two country roads and a deflection of a third bisecting one of these angles. Our line of battle, short as four small brigades front must be, could readily be turned on either flank by a larger attacking force. Do you understand, my prettice? If not, you will some day, and you can keep this letter and show it to someone who will understand.

Well, I made the best arrangements of which the nature of the ground admitted, placing W. H. F. Lee's Cavalry on the right, Ransom's and Wallace's Brigades, acting as one and numbering about nine hundred, on the left; then Corse, Terry and Stuart,

numbering about three thousand. Six pieces of artillery were placed at wide intervals. Fitz Lee's Cavalry
was ordered to take position on the left flank. About
two o'clock in the afternoon Sheridan made a heavy
demonstration with his cavalry, threatening also the
right flank. Meantime Warren's Corps swept around
the left flank and rear of the infantry line, attacking
Ransom and Stuart behind their breastworks. Ransom
sent word that the cavalry was not in position, and
Fitz Lee was again ordered to cover the ground at
once. I supposed it had been done, when suddenly the
enemy in heavy infantry column appeared on our left
and the attack became general. Ransom's horse was
killed, falling with his rider under him. His Assistant
Adjutant, General Gee, was killed. My dear, brave old
friend, Willie Pegram, was mortally wounded, falling
within a few yards of me, just after we had exchanged
'Good luck!' The captain of his — Pegram's — battery was killed.

I succeeded in getting a sergeant and enough men
to man one piece; but after firing eight rounds the
axle broke. Floweree's regiment fought hand to hand
after all their cartridges had been used. The few cavalry which had gotten into place gave way, and the
enemy poured in on Wallace's left. Charge after

charge was made and repulsed, and division after division of the enemy advanced upon us. Our left was turned; we were completely entrapped. Their cavalry, charging at a signal of musketry from the infantry, enveloped us front and right and, sweeping down upon our rear, held us as in a vise.

"Take this, Marse George!" said one of my boys earlier in the action, hastily thrusting a battle-flag into my hand. I took the flag, stained with his blood, sacred to the cause for which he fell, and, cheering as I waved it, called on my men to get into line to meet the next charge. Seeing this, a part of the famous old Glee Club, our dear old Gentry leading, began singing, "Rally round the flag, boys; rally once again." I rode straight up to where they were and joined in singing, 'Rally Once Again', as I waved the blood-stained flag. And, my own, overpowered, defeated, cut to pieces, starving, captured, as we were, those that were left of us formed front and north and south, and met with sullen desperation their double onset. With the members of my own staff and the general officers and their staff officers we compelled a rally and stand of Corse's Brigade and W. H. F. Lee's Cavalry, who made one of the most brilliant cavalry fights of the war, enabling many of us to escape capture.

WRITTEN IN DEFEAT

Our loss in killed and wounded was heavy; and yet, with all the odds against us, we might possibly have held out till night, which was fast approaching, but that our ammunition was exhausted. We yielded to an overwhelming force, Sheridan's Cavalry alone numbering more than double my whole command, with Warren's Infantry Corps to back them.

Ah, my beloved, the triumphs of might are tran⁄sient; but the sufferings and crucifixions for the right can never be forgotten. The sorrow and song of my glory⁄crowned division nears its doxology. May God pity those who wait at home for the soldier who has reported to the Great Commander! God pity them as the days go by and the sad nights follow! The soldier is done with tears and time, and to him a thousand years are as one —

Your
Soldier

Exeter Mills, April 2, 1865

XLI

On the Midnight before General Lee's Surrender at Appomattox

I WOULD have your life, my darling, all sunshine, all brightness. I would have no sorrow, no pain, no fear come to you but all

'To be as cloudless, save with rare and roseate shadows
As I would thy fate'.

And yet the very thoughts of me that come to you must bring all that I would spare you.

To-morrow may see our flag furled, forever.

Jackerie, our faithful old mail-carrier, sobs behind me as I write. He bears to-night this — his last — message from me to you. He is commissioned with three orders, which I know you will obey as fearlessly as the bravest of your brother soldiers. Keep up a stout heart. Believe that I shall come back to you. Know that God reigns. After to-night, you will be my whole command — staff, field officers, men — all.

Lee's surrender is imminent. It is finished. Through the suggestion of their commanding officers, as many of the men as desire are permitted to cut through and join Johnston's army. The cloud of despair settled over all on the third, when the tidings came to us of the evacuation of Richmond and its partial loss by fire. The homes and families of many of my men were there, and all knew too well that with the fall of our Capital the last hope of success was over. And yet, my beloved, these men as resolutely obeyed the orders of their commanding officers as if we had just captured and burned the Federal Capital.

The horrors of the march from Five Forks to Amelia Court House and thence to Sailor's Creek beggar all description. For forty-eight hours the man or officer who had a handful of parched corn in his pocket was most fortunate. We reached Sailor's Creek on the morning of the sixth, weary, starving, despairing.

Sheridan was in our front, delaying us with his cavalry, according to his custom, until the infantry should come up. Mahone was on our right, Ewell on our left. Mahone was ordered to move on, and we were ordered to stand still. The movement of Mahone left a gap which increased as he went on. Huger's battalion of artillery, in attempting to cross the gap, was being swept away, when I pushed on with two of my brigades across Sailor's Creek.

We formed line of battle across an open field,

holding it against repeated charges of Sheridan's dis-
mounted cavalry. At about three o'clock the infantry
which Sheridan had been looking for came up, completely hemming us in. Anderson ordered me to draw
off my brigades to the rear, and to cut our way out in
any possible manner that we could. Wise's Brigade
was deployed in the rear to assist us, but was charged
upon on all sides by the enemy and, though fighting
manfully to the last, was forced to yield. Two of my
brigadiers, Corse and Hunton, were taken prisoners.
The other two barely escaped, and my life, by some
miracle, was spared. And by another miracle, greater
still, I escaped capture. A squadron of the enemy's
cavalry was riding down upon us, two of my staff and
myself, when a small squad of my men recognized
me and, risking their own lives, rallied to our assistance and suddenly delivered a last volley into the faces
of the pursuing horsemen, checking them for a moment. But in that one moment we, by the speed of
our horses, made our escape. Ah, my darling, the
sacrifice of that little band of men was like unto that
which was made at Calvary.

It is finished! Ah, my beloved division! Thousands
of them have gone to their eternal home, having given
up their lives for the cause they knew to be just. The

others, alas, heartbroken, crushed in spirit, are left to mourn its loss. Well, it is practically all over now. We have poured out our blood, and suffered untold hardships and privations, all in vain. And now, well — *I* must not forget, either, that God reigns.

From now, forever only your

Soldier

Appomattox — Midnight — the night of the 8th and the dawn of the 9th

XLII

In which the General Tells of a Trip to Washington and of a Visit with his Old Friend Grant

SUCKLEY * and I arrived safely after an interest⸀ ing but, to me, sad trip, because of the many sorrowful memories that it brought back. Ingalls,† bless his old loyal heart, met us at the train and took us up in the Quartermaster's carriage. It is the first time that I have ridden in one of Uncle Sam's vehi⸀ cles since I changed colors and donned the gray, and now I ride, not as an owner, but as a *guest!* Again, my darling, there came to me memories of the 'has been' and 'might have been'.

"Well, George," said Rufus, "this looks kind of natural, doesn't it, old man?" But before I could reply, intuitively sensing what I was feeling, he continued hurriedly, "And this rig is at your service all the time you are here."

The three of us had dinner together. Pitcher,‡ whom you've heard me speak of as 'Old Jug', came

---

* Grant's surgeon.   † Grant's quartermaster.
‡ General T. Pitcher, U.S.A.

over from his table and joined us at dessert. After dinner all four of us went to the theater to hear Billy Florence. We sent a line in to him from our box, and when he came out he strode across the stage and, looking directly at us, said in his most tragic tone and manner: "The Lamb and the Lion shall lie down together," and then went on with his part. He knew, and we knew; but the audience didn't. He played to us, too, all evening; and never played better. After the play we went behind the scenes and had a charming visit with Mrs. Florence, who graciously gave her consent to Billy's going out to supper with us.

"And, by the way, General Pickett," said Mrs. Florence, "how is that beautiful Mrs. Edwards * with whom I saw you in Montreal, and with whom you were so much in love, and who, come to think of it, won all our hearts? Poor Ellen Tree was talking about her the last time I saw her. And how is that laughing bright-eyed baby who made a drum of himself and a prancing charger of everybody else's cane? I can see him now, with his mass of ringlets and his sparkling, laughing eyes. He had just learned to walk, and yet

* Edwards was the assumed name of General Pickett and his wife during their exile in Canada.

was charging the enemy on his fiery steed, beating an imaginary drum and blowing an imaginary fife. It was the funniest thing I ever saw!"

I told Mrs. Florence that we had returned to the States, that little George could ride a real horse now and beat a real drum, and that I was just as much as ever in love with 'Mrs. Edwards', who had become so attached to her assumed name that she hated to give it up and insisted that we should now and then call each other 'Mr. and Mrs. Edwards', to keep in memory the sweet, all-belonging life we spent with each other in Canada.

We had a fine steamed-oyster supper at Harvey's and told stories and talked of old times till after two o'clock.

I got up this morning just in time to go to twelve o'clock breakfast at the Club with Rufus. After breakfast we went, as arranged, to see Grant. I just can't write you, my darling, about that visit. You'll have to wait till I see you to tell you how the warm-hearted, modest, old warrior and loyal old friend met me— how he took in his the hand of your heart-sore soldier—poor, broken, defeated—profession gone— and looking at him for a moment without speaking, said slowly: "Pickett, if there is anything on the top

of God's green earth that I can do for you, say so."
Just then his orderly apologetically brought in a card
to him. "Tell Sheridan to go to——!" "Yis, surh,
I'll till him, surh." "And go there yourself!" "Yis,
surh, I'll go, surh." Rufus, who was whistling over
at the window, reiterated Grant's order, receiving
from the orderly the same assurance, "Yis, surh, I'll
till him, surh." While Sheridan was obeying Grant's
order and going to his new station, we three sat down
and had a heart-to-heart conference. One listening
would never have known that we had been on opposite sides of any question.

When I started to go Grant pulled down a cheque-
book, and said, " Pickett, it seems funny, doesn't it,
that I should have any money to offer, but how much
do you need?" "Not any, old fellow, not a cent, thank
you," I said. "I have plenty." "But Rufus tells me
that you have begun to build a house to take the place
of the one old Butler burned, and how can you build
it without money? You do need some!" "I have sold
some timber to pay for it," I told him. And to show
my appreciation and gratitude unobserved, I affec-
tionately squeezed his leg; when he called out,
"Rufus, it's the same old George Pickett; instead of
pulling my leg he's squeezing it!"

Grant is going to take Rufus, Suckley and myself to ride this afternoon to show me the changes since I was last here, years ago.

Tomorrow, if all goes well, I'll start back to what is worth more to me than *all* I've lost — my precious wife, who was as queenly and gracious and glorious as ' Mrs. Edwards ' in one room in a boarding house in exile, as she was in Petersburg in a palatial home, when her husband was the Department Commander, and she had not only ' vassals and slaves at her side', but the General Commanding and all his soldiers and our world at her feet.

Your devoted

Soldier

XLIII

After Refusing the Command of the Egyptian Army

S O, you would 'leave it all to my better judg' ment', most wise little one, and would not advise me; but after I had decided fully I was to read the mysterious sealed note — "Not to be opened till after you have decided."

At the banquet last night I opened and read the letter, and then passed it over to General E. P. Alex' ander, General Ingalls, and Doctor Suckley. They all shook their heads disapprovingly. I pointed to the instructions, "Not to be opened till after you have decided," and said that I had already decided and the note only showed that we are 'two souls with but a single thought'.

Now, don't you know, my darling, that I knew your opinion before, just as well as after, I had read your sealed letter? Of course I knew that you did not want me to go and that, as you prettily put it, "We've had glory enough, and war enough, with its hard' ships and separations and dangers, and now we just want each other forever and forevermore." Yes, my darling, we want each other, and a home, with a spiked fence around it, and a key to the road gate, for us alone, — just us, ' forever and forevermore '.

My friends all think that I am making a great mis/take in refusing this magnanimous offer of the Khe/dive. They hold that I am sacrificing my future, and signing the death/warrant to ambition and success. General Alexander has accepted, and will take com/mand of the Egyptian armies. Egypt could not have a finer officer.

Last night at the farewell dinner the Khedive's last telegram was handed to the Commissioner — "Forward Pickett at any cost." It was a most flatter/ing compliment, and I have asked permission to keep it for our boy. "The boy might think you were a brand of powder or a keg of nails," said Ingalls, who, by the way, is disgusted at my refusal. But, my beau/tiful wife, he has not you ; and love such as yours is worth all the gold and glory of the universe.

To/morrow I shall take the steamer for home with/out one regret for having decided as I have, — just you and I — just ourselves ' forever and forevermore ' —

Your

Soldier

New York

XLIV

In which the General Writes of Domestic Matters

IT is Thursday, and the cottage is so empty — so desolate, without you. Even Rufus feels the absence of its beautiful mistress and a few minutes ago, to show his sympathy for the lonesome master, brought and laid on my knee a little slipper which, if I did not know it belonged to my own fairy princess, would make me think that another Cinderella with a tinier foot had also forgotten the midnight hour. I gave no evidence of my appreciation of his effort to comfort me, so Rufus trotted off and brought me the other slipper. "Good dog," I said, "good dog," patting him on the head. Then fondling the little slippers and putting them beside me, I took up my pencil and pad to tell you all about it.

Presently, looking around, I saw Rufus planning to bring me everything in the room belonging to you. He has a lot of dog sense, and I tried to make him understand that the slippers had been sufficiently effective in consoling me; but he would not be convinced until I whistled our song, 'Believe Me, If All Those Endearing Young Charms'. Then, trying to howl an accompaniment and failing, he wagged his tail, lay down at my feet and went to sleep.

Every day when I come in to dinner, he trots up in front of your picture and barks till I take it down, then looking at it, barks again, while I encourage him, saying, "Tell her all about it, old man; tell her all about it!" When he has told you about it, he lies beside the picture, his paw on the frame, wags his tail and looks up at me till he thinks I have shown sufficient appreciation of his admiration and devotion to you; then he jumps up and points and barks at the place on the rack from which it was taken until it is duly kissed and replaced. Oh, he's a great dog, little one, and great company for me; but both he and I and everything else are lonesome for you, and we have promised ourselves that when you come back we will vie with each other in our efforts to make you happy.

Already the hens have commenced laying again. The butter is piling up to be made into cakes and good things. Your new little calf is a beauty — but I shall send him off and sell him before you get back, for you would never consent. The corn and wheat are beautiful, the vegetables fine. The flowers we planted all breathe of your purity and sweetness. The cutting

146

from the Poe rosebush which Mrs. Allen gave us is full of buds. So you see everything above the ground and in the ground at our Turkey Island home is waiting for your blessing.

This morning I took my gun and Rufus and killed five partridges and two rabbits. I gave one rabbit to Mr. Sims, and one to Uncle Tom. The birds I sent to Lizzie. As I was coming on home, I stopped and rested in the cool and calm of the forest, beside the old gray broken monument where we have so often made love and told each other fairy tales and wondered about and made thought pictures of our William and Mary Randolph, who erected it away back in 1771. I wonder, little one, if from their celestial home they can see the picturesque beauty which I see and which I wish I could put into words. Do you remember the inscription on one of the sides of the monument? — "The foundation of this pillar was laid in 1771, when all the great rivers of this country were swept by inundations never before experienced, which changed the face of nature and left traces of their violence that will remain for ages!" As I read over this inscription I feel sorry that the thought to erect a monument to commemorate any kind of disaster should ever have been born. Time's soothing wings bless always, and not only have the ravages of the flood which this monument was erected to commemorate been long ago forgotten, but the memories of ravages and horrors of a yester' day far, far more terrible are, thank God, being ef' faced.

The birds are nesting, and songs are being born, just where Butler's vandals mutilated and broke off the top of this monument, hunting for hidden treas' ure. Some of the seeds which the mother birds carried to their young have fallen by the wayside and taken root, and now out of the jagged, broken top grows a greenery of unknown vines and plants and flowers. The old colonial home of my forefathers, with its rare old mahoganies and paintings, which Butler sacked and desecrated and then burned, has been replaced by a sweet little cottage home built by ourselves, all our very own, and consecrated to love and contentment, with furnishings so simple and plain that we are not afraid of using them.

No, my sweetheart, we don't want any monuments to mark any of the woes and horrors of the past. We must build one of hope and faith and peace and mercy and joy, the foundation of which, love, is already laid in our hearts.

Listen — I hear old Sims' step on the porch. I hear

him knocking his pipe against the pillars — so, a Dios. He will tell me the same old stories over again, and I shall listen and laugh as though I heard them for the first time — dear old Sims.

Good night — sweet dreams. Angels guard you — while I hear of Lafayette and Nelson and Marshall, through the clouds of old Sims' tobacco smoke, for the hundredth, yes, for the thousandth, time.

Your lonesome

Soldier

Turkey Island

XLV

Concerning the Business Vicissitudes of a Soldier

YOU are always right, my darling Sallie, and your husband is only right when he is guided by you. Pretty generally he listens to his oracle, and when he doesn't he wishes to the Lord he had. The morning I left, when you urged that I wear the suit I had been wearing and I claimed that I hadn't time to change — "Then please take it with you and change on the boat," you plead. Well, dearest, I was stubborn. I wouldn't, and I didn't, and your obstinate soldier was not out of sight of the sweet lone figure standing on the wharf waving to him the love signals and the God-speed of our code before he was abusing himself as an ingrate in refusing anything that the dearest, most beautiful woman and the best wife in the world could ask of him. Well — 'dem dat dances is 'bleeged ter pay de fiddler', and your husband is paying — he is being punished, for he caught cold on the boat, had a chill, followed by sore throat and pain in limbs and back.

I stopped only a day in Petersburg to see our agent there, then came over here. At the Exchange, I went directly to bed and sent for Dr. Beal. He has been very attentive, coming twice a day. Julia and Wash took me in charge at once and, as usual, are as good as gold, and so is everyone, as to that, for each and all in turn prescribe a *sure* remedy and *urge* my taking it. Wash insists upon rubbing me with "turkentime, en den puttin' on a hot ingun poultice, en 'pon top er dat drinkin' a good hot scotch," declaring, "dey'll sho' en mingulate up wid one annudder en do de business en brek up dis 'fluenza dat's got 'session er you, Marse George. Doan you go projickin' wid doctor's medi- cines; pills is dang'us en dey ain' gwine ter oust no 'fluenzas, dey jes' gwine ter upset en sturbulate de bal- ance er yo' body dat ain' got de 'fluenza in it en mek dat part sick, too. Ef Miss Sallie wuz here she'd say, 'Wash, you suttinly is right — g'long fetch up a nice hot scotch, en git one fer yo'se'f while you's down dar gittin' yo Marse George's.' Lor', I knows Miss Sallie."

That settled it, and I compromised on the hot scotch — but I was firm and would not yield to Julia's entreaties to be permitted to bring me Mrs. Marshall's flannel petticoat to wrap around my throat. "What would the judge say?" I asked. "De Jedge, Marse George? — De Jedge ain' 'bleeged ter know nuttin' 't all 'bout it. Needer him ner Miss Sallie, nuther.

Dem whar's robbed, en doan know dey's robbed, ain'
robbed, Marse George, en ain' no wusser off," she ar-
gued — but I was adamant; her arguments were of
no avail. She 'curchied' her thanks for the silver
piece I gave her and left me with the compliment that
I "sho' wuz one bridegroom-husband — allus honey-
moonin' wid my own queen bee, wedder wid her er
widout her, en dat Miss Sallie ought ter be one proud
white lady." Is she?

Yesterday, when I wrote, I did not tell you how
sick I had been, or was; nor how lonesome; nor how
I longed for your soothing, gentle touch, your minis-
tering care. I should only have made you anxious. You
could not have come to me. Oh, my sweetheart, I
think of you all the hours, and I swear every time I
leave you, that I'll never leave you again and, that if
business calls, I must take you with me. If I could only
lay the treasures of the universe at your tiny little
feet.

But this business, I'm afraid, will not earn my
cough drops, nor your violets and, oh, it is such a cru-
cifixion! You don't know how abhorrent it is to me.
I spur myself on all the time with this one thought
— that it is, my darling, for you. The day I came up
on the boat, I took out two policies, one for $7,000 and

one for $10,000. The men were both old soldiers, be-
longing to my dear old division. One of them said they
had to run me down and almost tie me to make me insure their lives. You know, dear, I can't do it. I'd
sooner face a cannon than ask a man to take out a
policy with me. Your soldier is *nothing but a soldier;*
the war is over and he is no more account. The company tells me that my agents must do the soliciting,
but I'll feel like a thief to take a commission on what
they have worked for and earned.

Yesterday when I came through Petersburg I
went, as I told you, to our office. J. B. B., our company's agent, was sitting with his chair tilted back
—foot on the table, smoking a bad smelling pipe and
reading 'Macaria'. "Hello, General, hello," he said,
not rising. "Sent in six policies this week, old man."
"On your familiarity or courtly manners—which?"
"Neither, old man, on gall, gall, old man, gall and
grub. Come, have a drink — ever read 'Macaria'?"
With the most studied politeness and coldness I declined his offer and in my most dignified manner
asked permission to look over the company's books.
"Come, what's eating you, old man?" he asked,
bringing his chair down with a bang and slapping me
on the back. Then he profanely informed me that I'd

"have to unbuckle a few holes and thaw out, if I
wanted to paint the monkey's tail sky-blue."

Alas, little one, I am afraid your soldier isn't much
of an artist. He longs to give his precious wife all the
luxuries and comforts and everything that is beautiful — but he can't thaw out, my darling, and he can't
paint that monkey's tail sky-blue; and, sweetheart, it
makes him crawl and creep to be associated with art-
ists who can. I was wondering as I came over, whether
it would be better to send our boy to West Point — or
get him a paint-brush. We have time to decide that,
however, for he is just a little over eleven.

Here comes the Colonel and 'old Mistis'; and by
the way, everybody sends love and messages to you
and our boy.

Now, my own beautiful wife, don't be anxious
about me, and forgive this long, rambling letter.

Your loving, good-for-nothing

Soldier

XLVI

Requiem

ALL the way to the station, my darling, I was asking myself whether I was right in yielding to your solicitations and leaving our sick child, with all the resulting care and responsibility resting on your ever-brave shoulders. And once, sweetheart, after thinking very seriously over it I was almost tempted to turn and go back, when the appealing words of your voice echoed through my soul: " Even if I knew our child would die while you were gone, I would not have you neglect *this call* to honor your boys whom you led to their death!" So, instead of turning back I said: "Drive faster, please, John David; I wouldn't miss my train for anything!"—You blessed little sermon!

I made the train in plenty of time, and your mother, to whom I had telegraphed at Ivor, came to the station, bringing the good tidings that your brother was out of danger. I did not tell her that our little George was ill, lest it might make her anxious, as I knew that her duty was beside her sick boy.

I would have been so thankful if you, my sweet, beautiful bride, and our precious little 'war-child' *could* have come with me. Everybody asks about you and the boy and sends love, and expresses sorrow that you could not come. A delegation of my old soldiers met me at the station and, though some of our relatives had prepared to have us with them, I agreed to the arrangement of the Committee and the demand of the Governor and was taken to the Executive Mansion as the guest of the State.

All the evening and the next morning until it was time to form, old comrades came in, in groups and in single file. They told of their experiences, officers and privates alike ; discussed the Pennsylvania campaign and the three days' fight, their voices falling to a whisper as they spoke of those whose memory we had come to honor — our gallant dead at Gettysburg — our brave boys who gave 'their last full measure of devotion' to duty.

I had been made Chief Marshal — a sad, solemn, sacred office for me — of all the Army. Such love, such reverence, was Christ-born. You cannot conceive of it. From the old Market to the Cemetery

REQUIEM

of Hollywood, the streets, sidewalks, windows and housetops were crowded. There must have been twelve thousand people at Hollywood. Such a de⁄ monstration of devotion and sympathy was, I think, never before witnessed on earth. Think of it, my darling, so penetrating, so universal a oneness of love and respect and reverence existed that there was a stillness, an awesomeness, save for those necessary sounds — the clanking of swords, the tramp of horses, and the martial tread of men keeping time with fu⁄ neral marches — the solemn requiem. No cheers, no applause; only loving greetings from tear⁄stained faces, heads bent in reverence, clasped hands held out to us as we passed along. As I saw once more the cour⁄ age⁄lit faces of my brave Virginians, again I heard their cry — "We'll follow you, Marse George!" From their eternal silence, those who marched hero⁄ ically to death looked down upon us yesterday. My darling, you cannot know — no, you cannot know!

As I clasped the hand of one after another of those who crowded around me, I was greeted with the words — " My husband was killed at Gettysburg " — " My son is lying there among the dead " -- " My brother was with you there " — so many crushed hearts filling my heart with grief. Oh, my wife, my

General Pickett's Letters

Sallie, if the cry of my soul had been voiced it would have been the echo of that at Gethsemane!

Your heart-sad

Soldier

THE END